the green hill

the green hill
letters to a son

sophie pierce

unbound

FIRST PUBLISHED IN 2023

Unbound
Level 1, Devonshire House, One Mayfair Place, London w1j 8aj
www.unbound.com

© Sophie Pierce, 2023
Maps and illustrations © Alex Murdin

Typeset by Jouve (UK), Milton Keynes

A CIP record for this book is available from the British Library

ISBN 978–1–80018–180–9 (hardback)
ISBN 978–1–80018–181–6 (ebook)

Printed and bound in Great Britain by Clays Ltd, Elcograf S.p.A.

1 3 5 7 9 8 6 4 2

Felix Pierce Murdin
15/2/1997–9/3/2017

'He felt that in this strange place he was passing, while still in time, inside the bounds of eternity.'

John Buchan, *Sick Heart River*

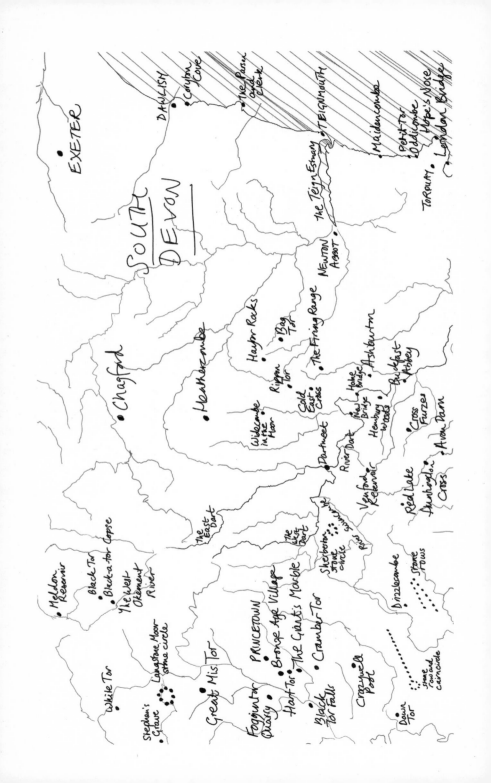

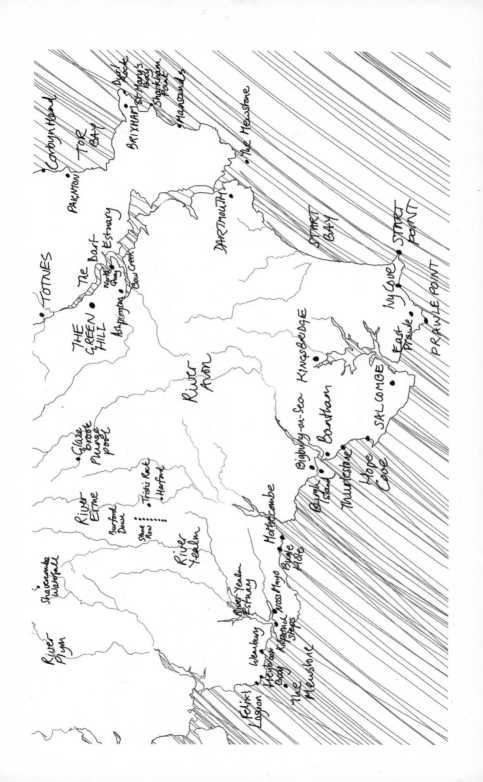

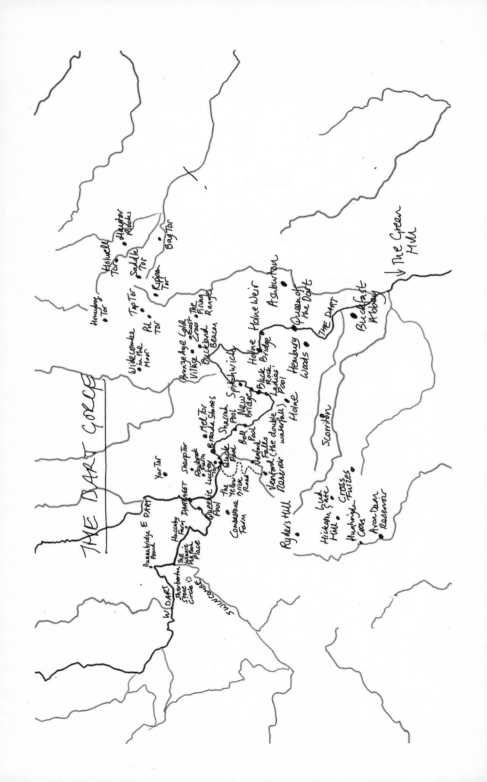

Contents

A note to the reader

My son Felix died suddenly and unexpectedly on 9 March 2017. He was twenty. Very soon after his death I found myself writing letters to him in a big red notebook. It was something I instinctively did. It was a way of dealing with the shock; I was pretending he was still there. I wanted to talk to him, I wanted to keep open that channel of communication, I wanted to express my thoughts, my grief, my anger, my disbelief, my rage and my utter devastation at his death.

Weeks and months went by, and I continued to write to him. The notebook in which I wrote the letters became a safe space, a kind of confessional, where I could explore my feelings and what was happening to me. Writing about my pain helped to dissipate it, and helped to give me perspective. It didn't solve anything, but it helped me get through each day.

The writing became part of my daily existence. As life went on, I started to wonder about sharing my thoughts more widely. The main motivation was to create a permanent memorial to Felix in a book, to have his name live on in my words. I was discovering that one of the worst things about losing a child is that their name is no longer mentioned in the same way that other people's children are naturally a topic of conversation as life goes on. But also, at a visceral, angry level, it was to tell the world, scream to the world: 'This is what it is like to lose a child.'

I also wanted to explore my grief, to try and understand it, and I felt it could be beneficial for others to read about my experience. Grief and loss affect us all in so many different ways, and are actually an intrinsic part of daily life. Grief is not always about the death of a relative or friend, but can also be about the loss of identity, of self, of ways of life, as well as more minor things. The climate crisis, the pandemic, and continued wars around the world all contribute to an existential feeling of grief.

As time went on, I found – as I always have – great solace in being outside, out on the hilltops and moors, deep in the woods, and in the water. I was surprised to discover that I didn't just find solace, I found joy. When Felix died, I thought I would never experience happiness again. What I found is that intense grief and intense joy can exist side by side.

When it came to turning the letters into a book, I felt that the letters alone would not be enough; I needed to help the reader get to know Felix and the story of his short life. So, the book is not just my letters to him, as well as an account of how the months and years unfolded after his death, but also my memories of his life, from a young child to a young man. In some cases, I turned some of the contents of the letters into a first-person narrative.

The book contains illustrations by Felix's father (and my husband) Alex. We hope they will enrich the text and build on the ideas expressed within.

When somebody dies, their existence ends, but the relationship you have with them doesn't. My letters to Felix became a way of continuing that relationship, which has inevitably changed. Gradually the letters started to become a diary of my life without my son; how my life continued and continues without him.

Of course, the final letter of the book is not the final letter I wrote to Felix; I have continued and will always continue to write to him. A book has to have an ending, however, so inevitably there is a final letter. But the story goes on, and will never be over.

Prologue

I am back at the green hill, far away.

The wind on the exposed hillside scythes my body. It always seems to be howling a gale up here and, as usual, I'm thinking, *What now?* I've been standing like this for a while, staring down to the still, silvery river, bordered by reeds and marshes, which winds through the fields below. Beyond it, under a heavy, grey sky, lies the sea. In the other direction, away to my left, is the lumpy outline of Dartmoor. I need to be here. But I also have to get away.

I head down to the estuary below and walk along the bank where wild garlic is emerging; there are no flowers yet, just broad shiny leaves and a faint oniony echo. Scarlet elf cups nestle in the moss. As I walk, the smooth surface of the river glints through the trees. Some geese pass above, their coarse cries reverberating. I reach North Quay, an old stone jetty that protrudes into the briny water. As I begin to change, a light breeze blows downstream, making me shiver. As usual, I leave my clothes in an untidy heap on top of my rucksack, impatient to get in. I walk across the ragged grass that covers the top of the quay, a feeling of dampness between my toes, and climb down the old metal ladder off the jetty. Its rungs are cold and hard on my feet. I sink backwards off it into the River Dart. The water is turbid but silky. The tide is going out and I swim upstream past the twisting oaks whose long boughs dip into the water like the arms of wizened old ghosts reaching for sustenance. Fronds of bladderwrack float by me in the water. I look up to the Green Hill high above, where I've just been. And in that moment, I feel myself fall away.

The 'Green Hill' is where my son Felix is buried. My brother James calls it the Green Hill Far Away, recalling the Easter hymn we used to sing as children. Tiny snowdrops appear there in January, fighting their way through the rocky ground and up through the graves. They are followed by primroses and daffodils, then poppies and grasses, legions of grasses swaying on top of the mounds, blown by the wind that travels in over the moor from the Atlantic. These flowers, these grasses, this smooth river that flows below the Green Hill to the sea, they are all beautiful distractions from the fact that his body is buried here. It is down in the impoverished, stony earth below, wrapped in an old linen sheet that I inherited from my mother. There are thirteen cowrie shells in with him, too, that we collected on Cornish beaches on countless holidays: one for every member of the family, to keep him company.

I continue to swim upriver, pushing against the out-going tide, trying to remember Felix's childhood.

Momentarily, I'm back in our tiny garden in Cambridge, years before all this happened. The apple blossom is out, pink-and-white blobs dotting the ground like confetti as Felix runs around the scrap of lawn, giggling. He's wearing his T-shirt with the dinosaur on. I'm lying under the tree listening as he screams with delight and huffs and puffs. The sun is warm on my face and I look up through the branches to the blue, cloudless sky above. We're having a heatwave. A large cardboard box lies on the grass, its flaps open and inviting. He goes up to the box, gets down on his hands and knees, and pulls open one of the flaps, revealing its dark interior. He looks inside and then back at me, questioningly.

'Go on! In you go!' I say.

He pulls open the other flap and I watch him disappear inside, making a great show of carefully closing the flaps behind him. Seconds later one of the flaps is punched open and his fist, followed by his face, appears.

'Ha ha ha ha ha!' he squeals, thrilled with his performance.

After this, a few more fleeting moments come back to me, but it feels as though my memories are suffocating in a thick sea of mud.

It's hard work swimming against the current. Being here in this river is both a penance and an act of worship. I need to be here: it is a kind of compulsion but also a distraction, an empty space where nothing has meaning or relevance; a place I can be absent. In the water, I shrink back to a sort of visceral essence of being, rewinding back to Felix when he was part of my body, part of me, grown from me.

Moving along the shoreline, I notice sea-green lichen all over the banks like mould on a cheese. It sits next to velvety moss, which grows on the exposed tree roots. The water ripples past me, gentle and soothing, making a pleasant sound. I put my face in, holding my breath. Nothing is visible underwater — all I can see through my goggles is briny murk — but the river is soft, poppling against my cheeks. Further up the estuary there is a marshy area where I get out, my feet oozing through the sticky silt as I walk towards firmer ground. Some ducks are visible in the distance and a huge weathered tree trunk lies beached on the shore. I sit on the trunk to rest, choosing a worn section, denuded of bark, a natural seat. Again, my eyes are drawn up to the Green Hill that overlooks the estuary. I can see the trees on the skyline and the oval cob building that sits at the top.

Not long ago we were gathered up there putting Felix's body in the ground. And a few weeks before that he was a young man just twenty years old. We were a normal family then.

Year One

A life ends

15 March 2017

Why? Why, why, why? Why are you dead? Oh darling Felix, the stinking cruelty of it — you cannot be dead. Why have you been taken from me, aged just twenty? Robbed of your future, robbed of love, robbed of your family, so young? I wish it could have been me, not you. I still can't believe you're dead. You cannot be dead. I AM SCREAMING, 'YOU CANNOT BE DEAD.'

This is grotesque — I cannot breathe, I am stumbling around, felled. I feel as though I've been hit by a ten-ton truck. One day you were there, we were texting, I was coming to see you; the next thing I knew was ambulance and police and officialdom and letters from the coroner and the involvement of the state.

What is reality? I really don't know. Felix, you are no longer here. So, where am I? I am your mother – I need to be with you, but you're lying in a fridge. I feel sick.

(A little later)
Oh my beautiful Felix. You're dead. And almost immediately I am struggling to remember your early years. I cannot bear it. I need to have your life clear in my memory. Memory is all I have. But my memory isn't working properly.

I do remember, when you were first born, we called you the Eskimo, with your dark thatch of hair, which promptly fell out, to be replaced with a golden crown of thick, straight locks. We have a few videos from your toddler years. You, aged about three, 'playing' the piano, screaming, laughing and turning the pages of the music every so often, as you had seen me do – even though you couldn't read the music, of course. Sitting in your high chair, breathing heavily as you excavated the last of the fromage frais from the bottom of the plastic pot, getting most of it on your face.

Thank God for these videos, because I seem to have such a tenuous grip on your early life. I desperately want to remember you, all aspects of you, all ages of you. Perhaps I can't because my mind is dominated by the horror of your death. This is all I keep thinking about. The horror, the horror.

It's two weeks since Felix died, and it's Mother's Day. I'm the first up, and come down to find Lucian's card on the kitchen table. No card from Felix. A total absence of him. An enormous void where he should be. The pain is deep, that physical ache of loss. Will I ever get over it? I have to. It feels like the most enormous task, a life's work, but what is life now?

My husband Alex and I go for a walk by the sea at Hey-brook Bay, to a section of the coast path we've not been to before, somewhere devoid of memories. Plymouth Sound, with its warships and great breakwater, spreads out before us. We get hot as we walk, as the sun burnishes our faces. Yellowhammers and coal tits dart about in the hedges, and there are gannets out at sea, dive-bombing, their wings black at the tips, as though dipped in a schoolmaster's ink. The hawthorn is out in creamy splodges, the sea is turquoise and we discover a rocky cove with a lagoon and a vast slab of rock to lie on.

The water is gin-clear and I swim, my head submerged, looking down at the white and purple rocks on the seabed below. I find myself crossing to the other side of the lagoon and touching the shoreline, a deliberate action, honouring Felix with a ceremonial placing of my hand on the stone. I find a large, smooth, white rock, puckered with lines of pink quartz like raspberry ripple, and hug it to my chest. Then I dive and place it on the sea bed, feeling myself falling downwards into emptiness. A boulder sacrifice.

A few years ago, Anna, a friend with whom I swim regularly in the River Dart, told me about an old man on Dartmoor who recalled a game he would play in the river with his friends as a child. They would dive down and find a pleasing, smooth and weighty rock on the riverbed, which they would grab and bring up to the surface. They would stand or tread water in the river, holding the rock under their chin, lean forward and let it pull them down to the bottom again, where they would drop it with a satisfying clunk on the granite bedrock. Since hearing about this, we regularly perform 'boulder sacrifices' while swimming:

contemplative and pleasurable, a small offering and a memorial. Until now the offerings have always been for my mother. Now they are for my son, too.

Memory has leaped in importance. This is the only way I can be in touch with Felix: thinking of him and the different stages of his life, maintaining his reality. But I find I can't rewind to all those different memories, those different experiences of him; they're drowned in a swirly, confusing mist in my mind. I have been told that grief affects you both physically and mentally; it is certainly causing the most acute brain fog. The loss of Felix makes me want to hold him in my mind and memory, complete, but it doesn't seem possible. It probably wasn't possible when he was living, but it didn't matter so much then. The strongest memories I have at the moment of Felix are of his death.

It was March 2017. I was driving to Leicester, excited about seeing Felix on stage in the chorus in his university performance of the musical *The Producers*. I hit some roadworks and pulled over to text him that I would be late. There was no reply; in fact, there hadn't been any replies to my texts over the previous few days but I didn't think anything of it. Normal behaviour for a young man at university with more things to think about than replying to Mum.

As I drove, I thought about his new life, away from home. He was in his first year of a degree in film, and loving it, having abandoned a previous law degree. That first attempt at university had ended badly; he hadn't enjoyed the course and had ended up seriously ill in hospital.

Now, things were a lot different. Felix seemed to be really relishing life, he'd joined the university theatre society and had been in a production of *Anthony and Cleopatra* the previous term. But the most important and precious thing to me was that he was making friends. His teenage years had been difficult – he had developed epilepsy and it had affected his confidence. He had become isolated and lonely.

I got to our meeting place and he wasn't there. I phoned and texted him with no reply and waited a while. Twenty minutes passed. I decided to try to find him. I knew they were rehearsing in a nearby building so I headed in that direction. Then I saw someone wearing a Leicester University Theatre T-shirt. 'Have you seen Felix Murdin? I'm his mum – I'm supposed to be meeting him?'

The student told me they hadn't seen Felix for a couple of days, despite a packed rehearsal schedule. He took me into the theatre, where the director of the show, Izzy, told me Felix hadn't turned up for the dress rehearsal. They'd been trying to track him down but they didn't know where he lived. I told them and they phoned the hall of residence to get someone to go and knock on Felix's door. The hall said they would call back.

I sat there for about half an hour, feeling an impending sense of dread but trying to reassure myself that all would be well. I sensed, though, that something was very wrong. There was no word from the hall of residence so I decided to just go there. Another of the students, Max, said he'd come with me. We got in the car; by now it was about half past five and the traffic was frustratingly slow.

Finally, we reached the Victorian red-brick building where Felix lived and I saw an ambulance outside his block. I felt absolutely sick to the bottom of my guts, a kind of animal fear, as though I was about to lose control of my bowels. I leapt out of the car and ran towards the front door of Felix's building. I could see an official-looking man in a shirt and tie standing on the lawn, talking on his mobile. He looked at me, aghast. There were another couple of men, dressed in black like bouncers, standing outside the door, and a female paramedic. They also looked at me with horror etched on their faces. They clearly didn't know what to say or do. 'Where's my son? What's happening?' I shouted. They looked at me and looked at each other and didn't say anything. I turned to the woman and, frustrated that no one was engaging with me, told her I was going to go inside and see my son, and she replied, 'It's not very nice in there – I wouldn't.'

I was about to push past her and go in anyway when a tall, broad paramedic emerged from the door. He looked down at me and said, 'I am very sorry. He's passed over.' I don't remember much of what happened immediately after that, but I do remember thinking 'passed over' was an awful phrase.

18 March

Since your death, letters have been pouring in. Every day there are more in the post. Everyone is so shocked, and many people have written such lovely things about you. Here's one I particularly like:

'I remember Felix on our school runs, and what an outgoing little chap he was, with a very inquiring mind. I remember thinking that he asked many more questions about all sorts of random subjects than my own brood. I have spoken to you, Sophie, about his words to my mother on one school run that really amused her:

My Ma (to Felix): So how was your day, darling?

Felix: It was OK. Why are you calling me "darling"? You aren't my mother.

My Ma (really laughing): I'm so sorry! I know I'm not your mother, but you are friends with my grandchildren, so I thought we could be friends too!'

And here's another one:

'There was a lovely occasion when Felix turned to us at breakfast and asked if we would like to come and stay with him at his home; he said that he had lovely toys. He then said, "May I come and stay with you? Have you got nice toys?"'

Oh darling (and I know I am the only one to be allowed to call you that), I miss you so very very much. I don't know if the reality of your death will ever sink in.

Alex and I are off to the Green Hill to visit Felix. It's about half past five, the end of a bright, clear day. The sun is setting behind the burial meadow and casting long shadows that echo the graves, pointing down towards the river. We walk towards his grave and see a freshly dug one right beside it; there'll probably be another burial tomorrow. The flowers on Felix's grave are dead. I remove them and replace them with a bunch of primroses from our garden.

We can see down to the river and on to the sea, where we can make out a boat. The bright red of the Devon soil in the ploughed hills contrasts with the bright green of the fields. We sit down by Felix's grave but it doesn't feel close enough. I lie down beside it and put my head on the grass above where I imagine Felix's head to be. I lie there with my face in the grass, smelling its fresh scent and looking through the blades. The thought of him lying below me is hard to comprehend and I weep. I continue to lie there, listening to the sounds — larks, predominantly, the odd seagull and then the coarse rasp of a pheasant. It is still utterly senseless that Felix is lying six feet under, buried in a Devon field, while life goes on all around.

The next day it is a friend's birthday and we head to the seaside at Bantham. We have tea and cake in her caravan, and I sit there, joining in the laughter but at the same time feeling desperate and hollowed out. Then we go down to the beach, where the sea is right out, and we surf in strong waves and glistening sun. My heart aches for Felix. I think of all those family holidays, bodyboarding together, shrieking with laughter as we sped up the beach on the same wave. I remember looking sideways at his joyful face as we zoomed along on about an inch of water. We used to hunt for cowrie shells, lying for hours on our tummies on the shingle, every so often the air punctuated by a shout as we found one. At low tide we would net enormous numbers of shrimps from the sandy pools. I can hardly believe I am here on this day out at the beach, just weeks after his death. It feels surreal.

That evening I feel very wobbly. It's the contrast between the celebratory mood of the day and what is going on inside me. I feel destabilised, trembly. I don't have much appetite for dinner. I'm exhausted and go to bed. I turn out the light and start thinking about Felix. My thoughts turn to him dying in his room, and I picture him lying there alone. My eyes and nose start to tingle and then I sob. It's not like crying I've ever experienced before. All words seem inappropriate: crying, weeping . . . no, it's more like howling, I suppose, mixed up with groaning and heaving. It's loud. There is an awful inevitability about it, like vomiting. It comes up in great uncontrollable surges from the pit of my stomach and I cry out in waves and waves of noise. Every so often there's a pause, and then it starts up again. A bit like having a seizure. It's totally out of control. Eventually it stops. I fall asleep through sheer exhaustion.

Memories of the day I discovered that Felix had died keep returning. Being taken to sit in the ambulance, where I was given watery tea out of a plastic cup. Sitting there on the gurney, surrounded by first aid equipment, phoning Alex and having to tell him Felix was dead. Worrying about how our sixteen-year-old son Lucian would take the news. Being taken into a wood-panelled room in a nearby building, where I sat for two or three hours with a female paramedic who was mostly silent but occasionally tried to chat. Not knowing what was happening. Staring down at my feet, clad in bright-blue trainers, as I sat on the sofa with my head bowed. Being interviewed by the police because it was a sudden and unexpected death of a healthy young man.

We had to arrange for Felix's body to be transported home to Devon. Once he was back, the undertaker brought us two locks of his hair and his watch, which was still going but an hour behind, because the clocks had gone forward. His hair looked darker than I remembered. I held it in my hand and stroked it. Then I smelled it and detected an unpleasant chemical whiff, which sent waves of horror, fear and revulsion through my body. It smelt of the mortuary and death.

We had to decide whether we wanted to see his body. The last time I had seen Felix I had been waving him off at Newton Abbot station as he left to start the new term at university. He'd been full of excitement and keen to get back to his friends; he was going back several weeks earlier than he needed to. We'd sat on the cold, hard metal seats on the platform talking about the term ahead and how much he was looking forward to being in the musical. As the train drew into the station, we hugged each other goodbye and I wrapped myself in his sturdy body. He got on board and I stood waving as he smiled at me through the dirty carriage window until eventually his face, and the train, disappeared in the distance.

I felt very strongly that I wanted to see his body but I was worried it would be too upsetting. Felix had been identified by his dental records. The coroner's officer had told us he couldn't be visually identified, but hadn't said why. What if he was unrecognisable, his face distorted and disfigured? It might give me a terrifyingly graphic, visual memory that would take years to fade. But if I didn't go and see him, would I be equally haunted by the images produced by my imagination, and also by the thought of not having taken the chance to see him when I could? In the end I knew it was something I had to do.

We were taken into the chapel of rest. It was just a room, with no windows and a waist-high plinth. Felix lay in an open coffin on the plinth. He was dressed in a cream satin gown tied around the waist with tassels, which looked like something out of a Halloween horror film. Some candles were lit nearby. His face was dark, mottled – black, almost. But it was unmistakeably him. It was Felix. He looked younger, child-like. And beautiful.

I gasped and sobbed and held his hand, which was deathly cold. His nails were blue. I stood holding his hand

and weeping loudly, breathing heavily. Then I stroked his hair. I wondered whether it had been specially combed to disguise where they must have cut his skull open to examine his brain at the post-mortem. I looked at his face – dark because blood had settled there, as he had been lying down when he died. I continued to hold his hand and stroke his hair, in a sort of trance of disbelief.

Then it all became too much and I sat down while Alex held Felix's hand. I reached for my rosary and started saying the Hail Mary and the Our Father, desperately clinging to my Catholic rituals, although I'm long lapsed. Saying the words was like a mantra that calmed me down, even though I don't really believe them any more. We stayed there for about an hour, holding Felix's hand, stroking his hair and face, unable to comprehend that this was the last time we would ever see him. It seemed wrong to go, yet what else could we do?

3 April

Oh my darling, your stuff came back from university yesterday. Your life in five cardboard boxes. Somehow so banal. Of course, your life is not about five cardboard boxes, but there was no getting away from the potency of those boxes. We slowly opened them, finding your clothes, your books, your games, your headphones, your notebooks. Each box had 'Fragile: handle with care' on it. We put the stuff in your room, and looked through some of it. We found your birthday cards, also postcards we'd sent you, including one from our recent weekend in Alicante. Then we found a sealed box, and in it was a card from the university Quidditch club and your team shirt, which you'd never collected. The shirt had 'Felix

Felicitas' on the back and the number 88. In the card, they said they'd retired the number 88 as a mark of respect.

I opened one of your notebooks and felt a frisson as I saw your familiar handwriting, with its elongated capital letters. It felt a bit like intruding, but I wanted to look inside, to touch the pages you had touched, the pages that held your precious thoughts. There were notes on the history of film, on the themes in The Third Man *and other films, and then I turned the page and came across an underlined heading: 'Ideas for Plays, Films etc'. I continued reading.*

> *Male/Female role reversal. In a country of men, the woman is Queen. Probably done before – research?*
>
> *Morality tales: criminals but the crime remains unknown throughout*
>
> *Train station – a man stops someone from committing suicide – play explores different roots of depression . . .*

My heart broke again. I never knew you were doing this. You were just starting to develop your ideas, to adventure into the world of the imagination. Who knows where you might have gone with that? This makes grieving very hard. I'm grieving for what might have been, what should have been. For all your potential, for your future achievements, for your future loves, your life. I feel what I have to hang on to is very formless and fluid. I have blurred memories of your babyhood, your childhood, your adolescence. You were different at all these stages. At the end of your life your identity, your character, was starting, perhaps, to coalesce, to form into a more defined essence, but it will remain fluid.

It is a month since the day I discovered Felix died. I wake before dawn, go down to the kitchen and sit with a cup of tea, feeling utterly lost. Sort of blank. Not crying; just sort of stunned. I decide to go and see him at the Green Hill, hoping to see the sun rise. But when I get there the whole place is shrouded in sea fog. I put my blanket down and lie there in the damp, looking at the grass on top of the grave glistening with dew drops. I listen to the sound of raucous birds. I can see three crows sitting on fence posts. I also hear the cries of pigeons, pheasants, and the odd flock of seagulls flying by; they are presences in the fog. I think about his body lying underground next to me. It seems barely credible.

Afterwards, I go to Torquay for a swim. It is a very low spring tide. Spring tides (nothing to do with the season of spring) occur twice a month, at the time of the new and full moons, when the water goes much further out and much further in than on other tides. Today, the sea is flat and blue, and I swim into and through the caves at London Bridge, a natural limestone arch. The exceptionally low water reveals shocking-pink jewel anemones tucked into the rocky crevices. Grey elephant-hide sponges and yellow encrusting sponges cling to the walls. There are also dead man's fingers – a white, soft coral that forms in clusters like dripping candlewax down the insides of the caves. Sunlight bounces off the cave walls and through the water, giving a backlit effect. I feel out of my body; out of my world; out of time.

Driving home, 'Happy' by Pharrell Williams comes on the radio and it really sets me off: I howl. Disturbingly, it has kicked off feelings of joy, making me feel desperately sad that Felix will never be able to sing or dance again. I'm hit by a forcible internal conflict between the light-hearted happiness of the music, and the pain eating me up.

Back home I look through our old WhatsApp messages – our little chats, both when Felix was at home and at university. Me telling him to do stuff: to make the dinner while I was at work, or to make sure he put on a clean shirt when coming down from Leicester to celebrate a family birthday in London. I scroll through these messages time and time again, pretending to myself he's still there.

Felix's funeral was to be held at Buckfast Abbey, a Benedictine monastery by the River Dart. Despite no longer being a regular churchgoer, I really wanted a Catholic ceremony, as the faith is part of my life, even if I am not sure what I believe any more. I was brought up Catholic; my mother converted in her twenties, although my father is Church of England. The Catholic Church is bound up with my identity, for better or for worse, and with Felix's, too, and I wanted the reassurance of the religious ritual, the words of the Bible, the grandeur of the church and its trappings, amid the chaos of my emotions and distress. However, Alex is an atheist, so we decided that the priest would not be present at the burial; for that we would create our own, separate ceremony, to say goodbye to Felix and lay him to rest.

Felix was to spend the night before the service in the Blessed Sacrament Chapel at the abbey. The immediate family would meet him there at half past five in the evening, to welcome him into the church.

The day before, my friend Milla had taken me up to Hembury Woods, an ancient forest next to the Dart, with the remains of an Iron Age fort at the top of the hill. Our purpose was to gather greenery and flowers for Felix's coffin. We walked along the grassy paths among the oak trees and bracken on the plateau at the top of the hill, looking for ivy, which we pulled down from the trees and hedges in great sprays. The familiarity of the woods was comforting. I thought back to all those times here with the boys. It was a favourite family spot for walking and mushrooming. Felix and Lucian were particularly good at spotting hedgehog mushrooms, which are creamy white and are often found in groups nestling in the leaves on the forest floor. I would send them off into the woods on either side of the path, and be rewarded with whoops of joy as they struck fungi gold.

After gathering a basket full of ivy, Milla and I turned our attention to the clumps of primroses dotted among the trees. As we crouched, picking the delicate stems, breathing in their sweet scent, I felt a sense of utter bewilderment at what I was doing.

The next day, before we were due at the chapel, I had a short sleep. After I woke, I became more and more anxious as the time approached to leave. In the car, as we got nearer, I felt waves of anxiety moving up my body. We arrived at the abbey and when I saw the hearse parked outside, I started to sob uncontrollably. That black car – so symbolic, so final. Milla was there to place the flowers on Felix's coffin. It wasn't actually a coffin, but a shroud made of cream felt. She had made a spray of the ivy, ferns, primroses, violets and wood anemones that we'd gathered. She laid the flowers on the shroud, which lay in the back of the car.

My three brothers Matthew, James and Ned, Ned's wife Kate and their children – my three nieces Tess, Ruby and Cosy – were there, as was my ninety-two-year-old father

Roger, in a wheelchair, and of course Alex and Lucian. We stood in the cold, grey afternoon by the vast Abbey, and the priest, Father Francis, appeared. The men were instructed how to carry Felix. They lifted him out of the car and we followed in procession through the abbey church, with Father Francis leading the way saying prayers and swinging a censer in front of him. The church was dark and silent, apart from the sounds of our footsteps on the marble and the clicking of the censer. We passed through the nave, with its marble side altars, a place I had been many times previously but in very different circumstances, before reaching the Blessed Sacrament Chapel behind the main altar.

The light was subdued and the incense was quite overpowering. A wooden bier carved from limed ash had been lent to us and was waiting in front of the altar, surrounded by large candles. Alex, Lucian, Matthew, James and Ned placed Felix on it. His baptismal candle, which I'd kept since his christening, was burning to one side. All this was against the background of an enormous, brash, kaleidoscopic, multicoloured 1960s stained-glass window of Christ at the Last Supper. Father Francis said some prayers and read a passage from Matthew's Gospel but none of us took it in — we were all sobbing. It was the shock of seeing the shroud, the hearse, the finality of it, the ghastly narrative of it all.

Huge, great, uncontrolled groans and gasps came up from the bottom of my stomach. They subsided and then started again with no warning. Father Francis finished his prayers and left the chapel. We all just sat there, sobbing. We sat for some time and then a few decided to go. I didn't want to leave Felix. I sat for a while longer. I went up to the coffin and kissed it where I thought Felix's head was, but I still couldn't leave. I sat for a bit longer and then James and I went and stood in front of the statue of the Madonna and said the Hail Mary a few times. I went back and gave Felix another kiss. I sat down again, got up again and kissed him again, until finally I felt able to go.

The next day it was the funeral. Alex's family arrived first thing: his parents Lesley and Paul, his brother Ben and his sister Louisa with her husband James and their children Frankie and Zoë, Felix and Lucian's cousins.

Again, as we started to approach the abbey, my emotions physically surged through my body and I knew I wouldn't be able to hold them in. As we drew into the car park, I could see lots of people had arrived and from that point on, for the rest of the day, I was totally overwhelmed. As we walked towards the church, I saw friend upon friend − reams of people. People kept hugging me, and I cried and cried. It was a relief to get into the chapel and sit there, looking quietly at Felix's coffin. I don't know how I bore it. I was overwhelmed by my grief, overwhelmed by people's love, overwhelmed by the magnitude and utter strangeness of it all. Here we were, saying good-bye to our son at the age of just twenty. How wrong, how terribly, terribly wrong that was − how unfair, how cruel.

Afterwards, the men of the family carried him outside and into the hearse, and we took him to Sharpham Meadow for burial − the place we now call the Green Hill. It overlooks the Dart Estuary, which snakes down to the sea. To the left are the granite outcrops of Dartmoor. To the right is the English Channel. There is a fire pit in the middle. A small fire was burning there with a thin plume of smoke winding up into the air.

We brought Felix into the oval cob building that stands at the top of the field and is open on one side, with views over the meadow and river. Family and friends read poems and tributes. Lucian played the piano. My heart broke again as he played 'One Summer's Day' by Joe Hisaishi, the music to the Japanese film *Spirited Away* – a film both he and Felix loved. Then it was time to put Felix in his grave. We carried him to it and placed him on the bier while straps were put in place under the shroud. As he was gently lowered in, I felt as though I was going to die. The pain was immense, surging through my whole body. We said our final words. I almost shouted mine as the wind howled around us. They were the words of committal from the Book of Common Prayer:

> For as much as it hath pleased Almighty God of his great mercy to take unto himself the soul of our dear Felix here departed, we therefore commit his body to the ground; earth to earth, ashes to ashes, dust to dust, in sure and certain hope of the Resurrection to eternal life, through our Lord Jesus Christ; who shall change our vile body, that it may be like unto his glorious body, according to the mighty working, whereby he is able to subdue all things to himself.

Shouting the words was the only way to get them out amid the tears. There was anger in there, too, definitely. Yes, God, you have chosen to take Felix from us but I'm not at peace with that, despite these words.

I looked down at Felix in his grave and felt a total sense of disbelief. We threw irises in, and earth, too. It was a beautiful sight but also profoundly disturbing. Our son, deep in a hole in a field, who was young and beautiful and gentle and my darling child.

After the wake we went back to check on him. His grave had been filled in and covered with green turf. The flowers that had been on his shroud had been placed on top of the grave.

After the funeral

8 April

Through our bedroom window I can see bright blue sky, the vivid green of the hillside opposite and the red leaves of the cherry tree. It is a beautiful day. And yet you are not here. It is just wrong.

The coroner phoned yesterday to tell us that further samples — lung tissue and blood — taken from your body had not provided any answers and so your death is being classified as SUDEP — Sudden Unexpected Death in Epilepsy. We will never know exactly why you died. In a way it doesn't matter, because your death is so sense-less anyway. Nothing will bring you back. It is just so bloody cruel. Epilepsy was your cross to bear and then it killed you. And you never complained, you never once said 'Why me?'

Why didn't it happen to me? I have epilepsy too. Why didn't it happen to me? Grandpa wishes it could have been him, not you. He's ninety-two, for God's sake. I have to get used to life without you but I have absolutely no clue as to how I will ever do that.

The next day, the post-mortem report arrived. The reality could not have been starker: the letter was headed 'POST-MORTEM EXAMINATION ON BEHALF OF HM CORONER FOR LEICESTER CITY AND SOUTH LEICESTERSHIRE DISTRICT. NAME OF DECEASED: Felix Pierce MURDIN Serial No: S705.17 (cjr.lc) AR0140.17.'

And if I haven't been convinced of the reality of your death, the report makes it crystal clear. 'The body was slumped between bed and desk, duvet wrapped around him – appeared to have rolled off the bed . . . the body was that of a young, white-skinned male . . . there was decomposition change to the skin of the face. The skin was green/black in colouration . . . Taking into account all the information it is my opinion that this man has died from SUDEP . . . those most at risk are young males (20–40 years) with a long history of generalised tonic-clonic seizures . . .'

The report says there were therapeutic levels of medication in your blood, which gives some comfort, in that it tells me you were taking your tablets. It's just a shame they didn't help you. Your epilepsy has never been very well controlled and it was a constant juggling act trying to manage your drug regime. What a dreadful hand you were dealt with your health.

What a lonely place grief is. It is a solitary lump in the centre of my being, I have to experience it alone, and that is very tough. Loss is a lonely business, a lonely, lonely business.

Today is Easter Sunday and I've bought Lucian an outrageously large Easter egg, far more extravagant than usual.

We attend Mass at Buckfast Abbey with friends – the first time we have visited since the funeral. There is a performance of a Mozart mass by the Abbey Choir and an orchestra, and as soon as the singing starts my heart stops, and I feel all the agony at Felix's death surging forward and I weep. The soprano who sang at his funeral sings the solos, her voice sublime, and Mozart's heart-rending melodies touch me deep inside, unlocking all the emotion lurking within – the sadness, the grief, the utter love for my dead child. I feel purged, cleansed. The music is so beautiful, it's a physical as well as emotional experience, the body expelling its feelings as the sound enters the ears.

After Mass we visit the Drizzlecombe stone rows on Dartmoor. We hike up the hill so we can approach them from above, and look down on them in all their magnificence. We pass through the Bronze Age village at the top, where there are some hut circles. We find the entrances, which point south-east, and imagine them as little thatched huts 3,000 years ago, with our ancestors living in them. We stand looking down at the three stone rows stretching out below – one with the highest terminal stone on Dartmoor, which is called the Bone Stone – and then walk towards them. As we get nearer, the Bone Stone looms above us. We walk quietly along the rows, wondering at their purpose. Then we turn off to find Shavercombe waterfall. It is a moss-lined bower hidden in a cleft in the rock, the sort of place you might find sprites or nymphs. The water falls in a silvery curtain, tinkling over the acid-green moss. We end the walk with a swim in a small weir pool on the River Plym where the water is surprisingly warm and incredibly clear. I feel happy: happy to be in the beauty of Dartmoor, happy to explore these resonating places, happy to be with friends, happy to be loved, happy to be in the cleansing water of the river. We have a delicious dinner of roast lamb and I feel cheered up by the whole day. Yet how can this be? How can I be happy? Felix is not here and he will never be here again.

He'll never be part of my life experiences moving forward. That is so hard to write; impossible to comprehend.

I wonder where Felix is now. Is he still alive in some way? I'm not sure if I want him to be or not. If he is totally 'dead', extinguished, at least there is no more pain, there are no more questions, no more . . . nothing. But if he is in some other form of existence, there are endless, pointless questions. Where is he? Is he with my mum? Is he OK? Is he happy? What is the nature of life after death? Will we meet again? But there will never be any answers, at least not while I'm alive. Perhaps when I die? It's just all unknown.

Felix had a difficult start in life. He was born by emergency caesarean section, following an induced labour. For the first twenty-four hours he slept in his cot while I spent the time in an odd high of both delirious wonder and exhaustion. The operation had been horrible, and I was in a lot of pain, but I was overjoyed. The first shock of motherhood came a few hours after Felix was born, when I tried to feed him. One of the midwives passed him to me in an attempt to 'put him on the breast'. After a half-hearted try – I, for one, just could not summon up any energy – we both went back to sleep.

On the second day, we had several unsuccessful attempts to get Felix to feed; I could not get him to 'latch on'. A succession of midwives came to try to help. Each one would try putting him in different positions in order to get him to suckle. With each attempt the pressure grew, and I started to fear the whole process – would I ever manage it? As the time approached to leave hospital, five days later, we were still having difficulties. Each feed was a trial. First, he didn't even want to feed (indeed, on some occasions he put up a real fuss when I tried to put him to the breast); second, it was difficult getting him into position; and third, it was hard trying to get him to stay there and really take in a decent amount.

Back home, things didn't seem to get any better. I spent my whole time trying to get Felix to feed, and each attempt seemed like more of a battle than the last. All he seemed to want to do was cry or sleep. I was reduced to taking off his clothes or changing his nappy to try to wake him up and get him to feed. He cried a lot – no doubt because he was hungry – and yet he couldn't feed. I started to dread the ever-more-frequent visits from the midwife and the health visitor, and the tyranny of the scales. They were obsessed with weighing Felix. At birth he weighed 7lbs 7oz; six weeks later he was half a pound lighter. I booked us in to see the GP, who took one look at him, rang the hospital and got him admitted as an emergency. I remember sitting, exhausted and tearful, in a cubicle, with him looking very small in the middle of an adult bed. One of the duty nurses came in and gazed at him. 'He's like a little baby from Ethiopia, isn't he?' she said. She was referring to his skeletal appearance, which I, as an inexperienced new mother, had failed to see.

We eventually made it up to the children's ward, where Felix was force-fed through a tube that was put down his nose. During a quiet moment I looked at the notes at the end of Felix's cot, and was shocked to see the diagnosis 'gross failure to thrive'.

Felix struggled at first against the feeding, which was distressing to watch, but after a few attempts he got used to it. For the first time, he started to experience the sensation of a full stomach, and so, I guess, started to have proper hunger pangs. As he started to feed properly, the tube became unnecessary and he took milk from a bottle. The downward spiral had been transformed into an upward one. We spent two weeks in hospital, during which time Felix caught a virulent tummy bug that set him back.

It was a difficult time. The children's ward was very noisy, and the patients had a huge variety of problems. Alex and I took it in turns to spend the night on a camp bed by Felix's cot. He gradually grew stronger, and eventually we were allowed home. He continued on formula milk and rapidly caught up with his normal weight.

20 April

Oh darling, today, despite the fact it's nearly May, there is an unseasonal frost on the ground which rather mirrors the cold, hard feeling I have inside me this morning. I just don't know what to do with myself. I'm going to have to find something or else how am I going to get through the day but it just feels utterly bleak without you. I miss you desperately. It's a strong, hard feeling deep inside me, like a twisted knot of torment buried deep within.

I have this feeling of numbness, of you drifting away, fading, like water through my fingers. I can't accept your death, I won't accept it, but clearly this is unproductive as there is nothing I can do about it. I have to find a way of recreating you in my life so you are still there but in a different way from before.

Yesterday we went to register your death. It wasn't the normal procedure as your death has to be registered in Leicester, where you died. So, we had to go to the council at Newton Abbot and answer questions and fill in forms which will be sent to Leicester. It was obviously just another day in the office to the woman behind the desk. She made no expression of sympathy and exuded not a scrap of warmth. It felt utterly surreal. Registering your death: I still can't believe it — the state's tidying-up of the tooth-and-claw process of death. Your death in black and white and registrar's ink.

As I'm on compassionate leave from my job as a reporter for the BBC in Devon, the days are free for me to do what I like. It is amazing how I can fill them up with doing pretty much nothing. Wake up, go and make a cup of tea, go back to bed, play backgammon on my phone, look at Facebook, maybe read a bit. Eventually get up, go down-stairs, have a bit of breakfast, tidy up the kitchen, wipe the surfaces, go back upstairs, lie down on the bed, play back-gammon on the phone etc., etc. Life is on pause. I suppose I have to get used to the 'new normal'.

It is a beautiful sunny day and I drive to the Green Hill. As I arrive, I see a large buzzard fly away to one side, fol-lowed by a magpie. I park and turn off the engine, listening to 'Jolene' by Dolly Parton, which is playing on the radio. *'Please don't take him just because you can.'* It strikes a bitter chord. I walk up to Felix's grave and lie down beside it, my arm over the mound, like lying like spoons. The sun is bright overhead, shining through the blades of grass up close to my face. Skylarks sing above us. I get up and water the primroses and snowdrops we planted the other day. A man appears with a hand–held mower and starts tidying up a grave – another mourner, a member of this new club to which I belong.

25 April

I had the most terrible dream last night. It was so frightening I couldn't get back to sleep for ages. I dreamed I came home to find the house on fire, ablaze. I watched it burn until the fire had eaten everything and all that was left was a shell. The meaning is obvious. My life destroyed, everything lost, gone. My home, my place of safety, has gone. You are my child, my home, part of what defines me and you no longer exist, you have been destroyed.

I'm also having flashbacks of the time I discovered you'd died. Sitting in that wood-panelled room, like being in a Victorian box, those panels surrounding me like walls of dread. Seeing the ambulance outside your building. On one of these flashbacks, I suddenly wondered what had happened to you while I was taken to the panelled room. I realised they must have put you in a body bag and taken you to the mortuary. The thought of your body in a plastic bag on a stretcher sent me off into another hideous crying attack, shaking with fear and revulsion at what had happened to you.

I also keep thinking about you lying dead in your room. I cannot bear that you died alone. It's such a haunting image, your body slumped between the bed and the desk. My mind keeps returning to this image, like a tongue to a space where a tooth should be.

*And yet another night I had a lovely vivid dream about you.
I dreamed you were alive again. We were at a summer party by
a lake, you were wearing your maroon check shirt you were very
fond of, and you were smiling and animated, chatting away. It
was so good to see you, as a happy young adult, which is what
you were starting to be.*

When Felix was about six months old my parents asked if
we'd like to go on holiday to Cornwall with them and the
rest of my side of the family: my three brothers and my
sister-in-law and my little niece Tess, who was nearly two.
Felix was over his difficult start and was at the baby blob
stage – not yet crawling, an adorable bundle that we carried around in a backpack. He was freshly minted, our
new treasure, and it was a happy time, our family newly
extended with the grandchildren Tess and Felix. We stayed
in a bungalow overlooking Daymer Bay on the north
coast, with a vast garden and within rolling distance of the
beach.

One morning Mum and I decided to walk along the
coast to Greenaway Beach, a shingle cove with striking
purple-and-green-striped rocks. I put Felix in the backpack
and we set off past the clouds of tamarisk that bordered the
path. We walked past a row of 1930s houses that reminded
Mum of her childhood, coming on regular holidays to
Polzeath with their family's boxer dogs. We have lovely old
black-and-white photos of them picnicking among the
rocks and surfing on their wooden boards. They used to
stay at Ivy Cottage, just up from the beach, and there is
another photo of Mum aged about fourteen, wearing a
cricket jumper, standing with her board by the house.

Mum recreated these childhood holidays with her own family, thirty years later. I have lots of memories of rock-pooling and bodyboarding in Cornwall as a child. Now baby Felix was the third generation of the family to be coming on holiday here.

We walked gingerly down the steep staircase to the beach, taking care to make sure we didn't drop Felix. Once down, we walked along the shingle to the far end, past a large rock pool that was a favourite swimming spot of mine and my brother James's as children, and where we had once spotted a large sea cucumber, which both fascinated and revolted us. We sat down and laid out a rug for Felix to sit on.

As Mum sat with Felix, I walked to the edge of the cliff, bent down and started to run my fingers through the shells and shingle. The best shells get thrown up against rocky surfaces and come to rest there. Limpets were everywhere, there were lots of yellow periwinkles dotted about like little jelly beans, and lots of pink-painted topshells. I got down on my tummy and looked even more closely. I spent about quarter of an hour poring through the shingle, before I finally found what I was looking for: a cowrie shell. With a great cry of triumph, I leapt up. 'I've got one!' I felt ridiculously happy. Finding a cowrie shell was a ritual quest while on holiday in Cornwall and I never felt things were right until I found one. The shell was ceremoniously shown to Felix, and I put it in my pocket to add to my collection.

The Green Hill

Last night I dreamed you were a toddler in my arms again and you looked into my eyes and said, 'Mummy.' Ah, that gorgeous physical relationship with you as a baby and small child, the fact that you had to be held and carried, the intimacy of touch and feeling your warm, soft body, hearing your voice and laughter, feeling your life force. You were delicious, with your soft skin and glossy hair. I remember the night of the Labour landslide in 1997 – you were three months old and I was breastfeeding; we watched the results unfold overnight, including seeing Michael Portillo lose his seat. You were a New Labour baby. Then I remember the day Diana died, a few months later, hearing the news on the radio while changing your nappy in our downstairs bathroom in our little house in Cambridge. That was our first home, and it was fairly basic; we'd done a lot of the work ourselves and I remember that changing table in the bathroom – Dad made it out of wood so that it could be slotted onto the top of the bath, so we could dry and change you more easily.

I have been struck by a line in a book about grieving for teenagers that I got for Lucian. It says, 'one thing that makes grieving such a challenge is that it can be hard to figure out who you are when a piece of your family puzzle is missing'. I wept when telling Dad about this line. It feels so true. As a family we all fitted together in a certain way. It certainly wasn't a perfect way, but we were a unit made up of four complementary parts. Now you are gone we are only three. What is our identity as a family now? What is my identity as a mother, what is Dad's identity as a father, what is Lucian's identity as a brother (and indeed as a son, as that has also changed, as he is now an only child)? Dad says laying the table makes him so sad: it's just three places. I had to write a birthday card to Grandpa just a few days after you died;

it was so difficult just to write 'love from Sophie, Alex and Lucian' and not to put your name. Your godfather Sean told me about a friend who lost a child — they sign their cards including their daughter as 'Angel Abbie'. I'd like to think of something similar for you. 'Angel Felix' — well, that's too cloying. I thought of 'spirit' but that's weird. There's no easy way: the fact of the matter is you're not here any more. Maybe something like 'love, Sophie, Alex, Lucian, and never forgetting Felix'. I don't know.

I am feeling so numb. I am thinking about the difference between grieving and mourning. We hear a lot about grieving but not so much about mourning. So, what is the difference? Grief seems to be more of a description of a state of mind, a term for something that happens *to you*. Mourning is more something that you *do*, something active. The modern way is to seek help with grief — to talk, to seek counselling. But I am more attracted by the idea of mourning as something active I can do for myself, allowing myself the time and space to be sad, and finding ways to do that.

It is also something I have to do alone. It would be lovely if, somehow, Alex, Lucian and I could mourn together, but it seems impossible. We are all in our individual channels of grief. We share a terrible loss, but we are also isolated from each other in our distress. It is just too much to discuss, to share. We have to concentrate on getting through each day, on focussing on survival.

My sister-in-law Kate has given me a picture book called *Michael Rosen's Sad Book*, illustrated by Quentin Blake. Michael's son Eddie died of meningitis aged eighteen. On the first page it has a picture of Michael smiling.

Below it, it says, 'This is me being sad.' I really identify with that. I can't go around with a long face all the time; I have to survive, to carry on. I have to play the game of life. But there also need to be private times when I can show my sad face.

I am starting to go through Felix's things. They are in his room; all that remains of him. I go to his desk and start to sort through all the papers, putting together anything with his handwriting on it. I look at his curly script, his thoughts translated into physical form. I hold the pieces of paper on which he made the marks, feeling an echo of his presence. I find his university pass, with his serious face in the photo, and take it and put it by my bed.

I sigh at the thought of his clothes. I take them out of the drawers, touching them and smelling them, that musty scent of him. He once inhabited these clothes; I've seen him in them and hugged him in them. I find a rather rude T-shirt he was particularly fond of, and an Amsterdam University hoody he wore a lot in recent months. I sort them out into clothes to keep and clothes to throw away or give to charity. There is a kind of hardness deep inside me that forces me to go through his clothes, making decisions about them. The idea of throwing any of his things away is impossible, but on the other hand I feel the need to order, even curate, what is left of him. I can't just let everything sit where it is. I am going to wash all the clothes I am keeping and put them back in his chest of drawers.

Snowdonia

7 May

My darling Felix, the wound of your loss feels so open and raw. Its constant presence makes normal experiences surreal. Last night I went to support a friend's fundraiser – it was a barn dance at Buckland Athletic Football Club (which incidentally serves up the most rank white wine; I have a terrible hangover today despite only consuming one glass). I took part in one dance, but honestly, it just all felt totally weird. Everyone was laughing and clapping and yee-hawing, and I felt so removed and detached from it all. A woman at the next table seemed to be staring at me and I found myself thinking 'Somehow, she knows' and feeling that your death has made me an object of interest. I hate that.

I can't bear the thought of all you are missing. At the weekend it was my friend Yaara's fiftieth birthday party. It was beautiful: the house and garden were lit with little candles in paper bags, the food was plentiful, colourful and delicious, and all our friends were there with their delightful teenage and adult children. You should have been there, like you were less than six months ago, at New Year, in that very same house. I was so struck by how beautiful the young people were, and the harsh pain of your absence.

Every morning I wake up and think, 'Felix is dead.' It's that grim realisation that it wasn't actually a bad dream: this is REAL. We're so used to being able to sort out problems in life, being in control, even when things go wrong. This is the antithesis of that. We can't bring you back. We can't change anything. You're dead. That is the stark reality.

I have started reading A Grief Observed *by C. S. Lewis. He writes: 'I have no photograph of her that's any good. I cannot even see her face distinctly in my imagination.' I so understand that, even though we are lucky to have lots of photos of you. I cannot see your face distinctly in my imagination. Photos are a great aid to memory, but the thought that there will never be any more photos of you is impossible to accept.*

I am setting off on a retreat to my old university friend Candy's cottage in Wales, where we have had many holidays over the years. I am going alone – I want some solitude – though Candy will join me in a couple of days. The house is the prettiest wooden cottage overlooking the Mawddach Estuary, halfway between Barmouth on the coast and Dolgellau inland. It has a river running through the back garden, perfect for a morning dip. It is surrounded by the mountains of Snowdonia, and as I get in the car, I think about some of the places I will probably revisit during my stay – my old haunts, where I've been going since my twenties: Llyn Cau, Cadair Idris and the Blue Lagoon at Friog, to name a few. It's a magical place with many happy memories from my young adulthood, visiting with friends and various boyfriends, through to marriage and family.

I drive up through all those quaint Welsh border towns that time seems to have forgotten: Crickhowell, Builth Wells, Talgarth. Much of the time I am next to the River Wye, which is at times slow and lazy through fields, at times running fast over rocks. Then gradually the mountains start to appear – those magnificent Welsh mountains. Candy's cottage is waiting – a box of memories, full of connections to my past and reassuringly familiar. Everything's the same, just a bit smarter and more comfortable. The same William Morris-patterned sofa and armchairs, the same black-and-white photos of the family, the same kitchen with its ancient fireplace, the same green, lush garden with its waterfall and pool, where I immediately go for a refreshing plunge.

Over dinner I read the visitors' book, starting at the back, and immediately find an entry from Felix, which stops my heart. It says:

13 Aug 2009. Had a lovely time climbing Cadair Idris. Next day I cycled 15 miles. And the day after that I walked to an old quarry and watched Mum, Lucian and Candy swim. Felix Murdin FELIX MURDIN

That was such a lovely holiday. We fried sausages on our portable stove after that swim. I'll never forget that.

Candy took us to the top of the nearby hill and we cooked our lunch overlooking the sea and mountains. I remember thinking, *This is pretty awesome. How often do you have a view of the sea AND mountains?*

It is good to be here, a place with memories of Felix but also from before he was born, and from before I met Alex. I first came here as a young woman, when I was about twenty-one and at university, where I met Candy. I've been here with many different people over the years and it's always been a place of peace and refuge.

It is like high summer, with the sun beating down as I begin my climb up Cadair Idris, whose name translates as the Giant's Chair. I'm heading for a lake that sits in a crater behind the mountain. The lake's name is Llyn y Gadair. I'm taking the easiest route, the Pony Path, but I get hotter and hotter as I climb higher. The path is uneven, with lots of loose stones, and occasionally I trip. I know the lake is up ahead but I cannot see it. As I approach each ridge, I expect to see it, but am disappointed. Finally, I crest what seems like the hundredth ridge, and there it is, a glittering pool with the sheer cliff of the mountain rising behind. I get closer and see the water shimmer. It is so clear, and the most beautiful petrol blue. I can't wait to get in, to lose myself in its sheer size, to feel like an atom or an amoeba in the great scheme of things. I find a place to sit among the stones that surround the lake, and get changed into my swimsuit. I pick my way over the rocks towards the water and stick my feet in. The water temperature is a great shock – it's freezing, even for me. The water is vice-like on my hands and feet, so much so that I can't stay in for long, just a couple of minutes. The mountain is putting me in my place.

I get out and sit by the lake, overcome by a sense of isolation in this dramatic landscape that is strangely helpful and brings physical form to the way I am feeling inside. My surroundings reflect my state of mind.

I think back to previous visits to Cadair Idris, and in particular to an ascent from the other side, with Alex, Candy and the boys when they were about eleven and eight. Setting off from the car park and up through the twisted trees of the mountain's foothills, following a pavement-like path that then turned into slippery scree. Hoisting the Devon flag when we reached the top, where we could barely see ourselves in the mist. Sliding in the scree as we made our descent.

I think about epilepsy and its role in the lives of Felix and me. I had had my first seizure at the age of twenty-eight, which came as a huge shock at the time. I was living in Cornwall, studying at Falmouth School of Art, where I was doing a postgraduate diploma in broadcast journalism. The course was very hands-on and practical; we had our own studio and right from the beginning we made our own news broadcasts and programmes. For one particular assignment I stayed up all night with my friends, perfecting it before going 'on air' at 10 a.m. After the show, which went brilliantly, I came out of the studio and immediately collapsed. The next thing I remember is coming round and seeing all these faces above me, including a man I didn't know, who turned out to be a doctor they'd called out. He told me I'd had a seizure, and I was devastated. Throughout the course, we'd been told time and time again by our tutors that we *must* get a driving licence if we were to have any hope of getting a job. The first thing that happened after my seizure was that my driving licence was taken away.

I had various tests on my brain and everything was normal, as it is with the vast number of people who have epilepsy. In most cases there is nothing discernible that is wrong; it is just a condition you have where the brain misfires due to a sudden burst of electricity. For some people this might happen just once in their life; for others, it is a few times a year; for the really unlucky ones, it happens all the time and is a real curse. Triggers can be tiredness and lack of food – both of which applied in the case of my first experience. After a tonic-clonic seizure – the full works, with limbs and body juddering and jerking – you feel absolutely awful. Your muscles ache, your tongue may be sore if you've bitten it, and your head feels as though someone's stuck a screwdriver through your skull and had a good dig around in your brain.

Epilepsy is one of the most common neurological conditions in the world. There are around 600,000 people in the UK with it – at least 1 in 100 people – and there is often a genetic element. After I had my seizure, my mother remembered that epilepsy had been listed on my grandfather's death certificate. We asked my grandmother about it and she said, 'Oh yes, he used to fall down.' And yet this was never talked about or acknowledged in the family.

The next day I visit Shell Island, a little further north up the coast from Barmouth. I have always been curious about it – it sounds so romantic. Instead, it turns out to be quite a strange experience. I drive across a tidal road – a strip of tarmac across mud flats – past an airfield, to get to the 'island', which isn't really an island in the sense you'd imagine. It's a section of land along the coast that gets cut off at high tide. Most of the land is covered by a campsite on a mound of grass overlooking the sea, complete with pub, supermarket and shops. I walk past all these to find the beach, which is certainly not the prettiest I've seen, with lots of dark, gloomy boulders, but the sea is very blue.

I am walking along the shore when the sound of my feet crunching makes me suddenly clock the abundance of shells underfoot – scallop shells, oyster shells, cockle shells, mother of pearl, spiralled cones, all in an array of colours. I stop and sit down, and start to sort through them, picking out the ones I like. Despite the diversity, I don't find any cowries. I find a large flat rock and arrange the shells into patterns, grading them by colour and size, creating order out of chaos, or rather, creating a tiny oasis of order in my mad, chaotic, incomprehensible world. My mind slows down as it focuses on this small, creative task.

Here I am, alone on this beach, looking out on an endless sea, playing with shells. No one knows where I am. I feel calm and strangely content, sitting here, looking at the shapes, colours and patterns of the shells, thinking about Felix. I get up and start walking again, constantly looking underfoot. There is a lot of mother-of-pearl, glittering in the sun, and I find two pieces shaped like hearts.

I want a swim but the tide is way out. This means a tricky clamber over a strip of ugly black boulders that stand between me and the sea. Once over the rocky barrier, I find the water is shallow, brown and opaque, nothing like the initial stretch of blue I saw from the shore. I have to wade for a while before it is swimmable. There is no one about at all. The view out to sea is vast. I suddenly feel frightened and start to wade back in. As I make my way over the boulders and back to the shingle, I feel a sense of total alienation. I am alone in this strange, unfamiliar place and my son has died. I want to get back to the cottage, to familiarity.

I get back to find Candy has arrived. How many times have we been together at this cottage? I think back to weekends in the 1980s, when we were students: groups of us coming here, having long walks in the daytime and drunken dinners in the evenings. Long nights sitting at the kitchen table round a flickering candle, putting the world to rights and listening to cassette mix-tapes.

After some tea, we head out to the Blue Lake, which Felix talked about in his visitors' book entry. It is a turquoise pool of water in an old quarry that you get to by climbing up a steep hill and then walking through a tunnel in the side of the mountain. So, effectively, you are swimming in a pool inside a mountain. The late-afternoon sun is on part of the pool and the water is very clear. We swim and talk. Somehow the fact that we are talking in this place is helpful. It is somewhere we have been many times; it is a place of memories, of happy memories, a place Felix has been. Just a few years ago, Felix, Lucian and I were here, with Candy, jumping and diving in this extraordinary piece of water.

On the way back we stop for a drink at the George III hotel, which is right on the Estuary. We sit on a wall overlooking the water, watching the sun go down and illuminating the swirls of the river as it bends around the sand bars. The familiar wooden toll bridge (20p to cross on foot), with its white parapet, is to our right, and to the left is a promontory with pine trees; in front of us are the mountains. We talk. We talk about Felix, we talk about grieving, we talk about our families, our lives, in a relaxed way, a way you can talk only with an old friend. It helps.

The next day we go to a river just north of Dolgellau that is packed with pools and waterfalls. It is the most invigorating sequence of gushing, vital water, all cascading out of white-and-grey rock the colour of humbugs. At the top is Black Falls, an enormous pair of waterfalls, one on top of the other, that together are the height of one, maybe even two double-decker buses. We swim in the large pool below the bottom waterfall and I get right up close to the thundering curtain of water, feeling its powerful energy in my face. All those tiny droplets fizz in the air around me as I tread water with my eyes closed, held in a point in space and time, paused in this ancient landscape that has not changed for millennia.

When Felix was three, we relocated from Cambridge to Devon, wanting to exchange the flat of the fens for the moor, hills and sea. We moved into an old house in the stannary town of Ashburton on the south-west edge of Dartmoor. It was a bit of a gamble as we knew no one, and also had never lived in a small town before. But it turned out to be a great community and we could not believe the beauty right on our front door. We could walk 50 yards down the road and ascend a granite staircase in a wall that led to a field called the Terrace, where we could walk up to admire views across Dartmoor and down towards Ugborough Beacon. From there we could descend to the bubbling River Ashburn and walk along to the woods – packed with bluebells and wild garlic in the spring – and then walk back along the lanes past the Coffin Mill, an unusual house shaped like a coffin, or, perhaps less frighteningly, an iron on its side. What a contrast to a small terraced house in Cambridge.

Six months after we arrived in Devon, Lucian was born. I suffered from postnatal depression and I have often wondered what impact that had on Felix, who was only a toddler. My memories of this time are mercifully not that strong, but I remember a couple of terrifying episodes, when I was planning my death. I cannot have been a great mother at this time as I was only existing at a very basic level, trying to survive. I know the illness wasn't my fault but I feel so distressed and guilty about the effect it must have had on Felix. My mother came down to look after me and I also went to stay with her and my dad, and after about six months I was over the worst.

A couple of years later, Felix started primary school. His exercise books make for some amusing reading. In 2003, aged six, he was set the task of 'Writing Instructions: How to change for PE'. His answer was brief:

First, get your shirt and shorts off.
Second get PE shirt and shorts on.
Third get in line.

An appropriate answer, I feel, for such an uninspiring exercise.

Another task was to write a story called 'The Walk'. This was Felix's effort:

Once in a house there were children and mum and dad.
Then they went out. Then they got to this other house. Then
they went back.

Clearly, he could have made more of an effort with this, although the picture he drew is rather good!

When Felix was about eight, he decided he wanted to do netball. Netball was only played by the girls. But he wanted to do it and so he did. I was so proud of him for that. He wasn't afraid of being different. I remember him in the red bib and static-attracting nylon shorts, and taking him to a school in Newton Abbot for a match. He had a delightful teacher, who encouraged his interest. He played various matches at other schools and enjoyed it despite the fact that many of the boys teased him for getting involved in a girls' game. But after a while, the teasing became too much and he stopped.

Bullying started to become a frequent occurrence at primary school. As a parent, you wonder, *Why do others pick on my child?* He was a gentle soul and awkward at times. This was something that recurred throughout his school career and I found it deeply upsetting. He never complained but it did start to affect his behaviour. It made him more cautious, more reserved, more unwilling to take a risk.

What is it about a personality that encourages cruelty? Actually, that seems the wrong question to ask. A better one would be, why are people cruel? This has haunted me since Felix died. When I'm really low, I feel desperately sad that he suffered bullying in his short life, and I feel that his life was sad and then he died. Surely this cannot be the reality? I can't bear it to be the reality. Rationally, I know that this is not the case; that he was loved, so truly loved. But he suffered. I can't seem to escape that reality. I don't want to remember it, but I do.

In a school Easter play one year, he played Judas. I dutifully provided the costume of standard-issue tea towel on the head secured with a cord and a white robe fashioned from one of my grandad shirts, which came down to below his knees. As I watched in the audience and we got to the part of the play where he stood in shame, I wept. It seemed so cruel, given the bullying at the time, that he got the least cool part. I want my memories of him to be reassuring and happy but they are not. I can't rewrite history in my head, but why can't I remember the happy times?

10 May

I am back home from Wales. You are the first thing I think about when I wake up and the last thing I think about before I go to sleep. Yet I feel I am losing my grip on you, that you are moving away from me like an untethered boat on a receding tide, being taken away, fading into the distance. I want to hang on to you, but inevitably you will fade and I cannot accept that. There is a duality about my life now. On the one hand there's normality, keeping going, doing stuff, mechanically. On the other there is my grief for you, which is dominant, ever present. It is the only thing that has meaning or relevance at the moment. These two lives are running in parallel and it feels very odd. And yet I am managing – I am sleeping, getting up, eating. But this is life at a very basic level.

I've been going through your stuff and found a poster you had in your room in Leicester that I hadn't seen before: a black-and-white image of construction workers in New York having their lunch on a girder of a skyscraper, their legs dangling above the city below. It turns out it is a very famous picture, taken to promote the newly built Rockefeller Plaza in 1932. Your poster is a bit dog-eared, so I'm going to get another and get it framed. It will be a reminder of you. Not that I need reminders.

I walked into town the other day and bumped into a friend who I don't know very well. We chatted and she asked me how I was and I just didn't want to talk about it but of course I did, to be polite. It was weird; I was sort of floating above myself, hearing the words coming out of my mouth – just something to say, to fill the space. Then I went into the post office. They'd obviously heard, and Jackie the postmistress held my hand over the counter. Of course, I lost it and was standing there in the middle of the post office crying. This just has to be faced, though; I cannot spend the rest of my life as a recluse. I am glad word is getting out; it's better that people know.

Dad and I had another tricky incident a couple of weeks ago, just before your funeral, when we bumped into an acquaintance. She obviously didn't know, so we were there making small talk in the middle of the street and I couldn't bear it. So, eventually I just told her and the shock on her face was so stark – her face was the picture of absolute shock and horror. It's just an impossible situation for everybody really. All the people we come into contact with are trying their best. No one knows how to deal with the situation.

Follow the Yellow Brick Road

11 May

Darling, today I went to see you at the Green Hill again. There were two gravediggers busily working away all the time I was there. As always seems to be the case when I visit, the weather was quite volatile, with big clouds moving around but bright sunshine also. There was a guy with a small digger and another one manually marking out a new grave and digging away the topsoil by hand. Before I got to your grave I stopped to chat with him and he explained how he used to dig all the graves completely by hand but the ground is so full of rocks he was starting to hurt his back. He asked why I was there and I explained that I was coming to visit you. He said how sorry he was and I felt quite tearful.

I went over to your grave and the bunch of buttercups I brought last time was still there. I removed them and put a single red rose in their place, a beautifully scented rose from the bush by the front door, dark and velvety. I sat down by your grave and noticed that lots of different grasses are starting to appear. It seems important to give them names so I've looked them up: meadow grass, Timothy, various different fescues – and a solitary buttercup. The wind dropped and the sun came out, and I lay down by your grave and shut my eyes. The sun was really quite hot on my face. I could hear lambs bleating and the odd seagull, and I thought of your body beside me, underground, decaying. It's now over two months since you died. I wondered if your skin is still intact? Or has it decomposed? All the while, the two gravediggers were chatting to each other about this and that – how one had a leak in his radiator; the relative merits of the different engine sizes of Discovery 4 x 4s. Then they started the digger up and soon had a vast mound of soil, some of which they removed. So, it wasn't exactly a contemplative visit to you this time, but in a funny way it was quite nice they were there doing their work: the cycle continues.

Two months have gone by and your headstone is not yet in place. It was ordered ages ago. All the headstones are the same; these are the rules. A rectangular piece of slate with the name and the dates, carved by the same stonemason. I want the marker to be there. I want your name to be in place. This is very important to me.

Afterwards I drove down to North Quay and had a delicious swim despite the fact that the water was pretty brown from all the rain. It was warm, and I swam upstream to where I could see the burial field and blew you a kiss. I swam from one side of the river to the other, and then moved along close to the bank with its overhanging trees. I saw something white on the surface ahead.

As I got closer, I could see that it was a pristine white feather, curled up at each end, like a small boat floating along. Then a beautiful wooden sailing boat passed me — a big one with a cabin, powered just by the wind, the sails cracking as the boat moved by. Then, up from Dartmouth, came a motorboat, and after that a group of seven red and turquoise wooden open canoes with some loud teenagers on board. All the time I quietly observed from my position under the trees, hidden as the boats went by, just moving gently around in the water for no other reason than that I like the feeling of being suspended there, in time and place, paused.

It is a sunny, bright day, and Alex and I go to visit Venford Falls, a double waterfall that appears out of nowhere on a little stream down to the River Dart, its height out of keeping with the size of the stream. You can quite easily miss it as you walk by, as it turns away from the path, keeping itself hidden. The twin curtains of water crash down about ten feet into a pool below.

The sun comes out and shines through all the droplets of water that zing off the waterfall and we stand there, breathing in the energy that pulsates from this small bit of Dartmoor. The last time we were here was in January, just a few months ago. It was probably one of our final family walks, just before Felix returned to Leicester for the last time. It was freezing. I remember him standing under a fallen tree that frames the view of the falls. I wish he was here now.

We follow the brook down to the Dart and then head off upstream, treading ground new to us. Why have I never been here before? I don't understand it — it's so near home and yet, somehow, I've missed this place. Below us the Dart churns and foams, and the path disappears at times. Mossy rocks and leaf debris are underfoot as we make our way through the trees, which are bursting into life with young, neon-green leaves. We emerge on a bluff, high over the river, and then come to another promontory, which stands over an enticing pool below. We can see Luckey Tor and Sharp Tor on the other side and have an uninterrupted view up the gorge. We decide to try to get down to the pool, and follow the path downhill to a clearing, where there are the remains of a campfire. We then double back and bushwhack our way through undergrowth until we are under the promontory and by a magnificent round black pool with a bubbling cascade. We stand on a rocky platform beside the pool, and the water is just so tempting. I get changed and plunge in, and am sucked by the current down to the end of the pool, whirling around and down. The sun bounces down onto the surface of the water and through my goggles I see shafts of light hitting the boulders on the riverbed. I search for a suitable boulder to cradle. I find an oval, quartz-pocked one, and dive down to get it. I surface, gasping, and then let it pull me back down under. I drop it back to the bottom with a clunk. The sun sparkles through the water.

I am returning to a childhood state, one where I had no responsibilities and had not yet learned to love, and therefore had no idea about loss. It is a moment of non-me, of nothing, of loss of self. And yet in this moment I feel connected to Felix, as he has been lost too. He is no longer here, and in a sense, neither am I.

After, we find another track, which takes us back to the top of the moor, back to where we started. It curls its way up a valley, and halfway up I look back. The track winds enticingly down towards the river, and for some reason I christen it the 'Yellow Brick Road'. I feel it will be a sort of fantasy walk for me in future, taking me to a new world, where Felix does not exist, at least not in this temporal world but in a new location in my mind and in my surroundings. Maybe it is good to find new territory, new places that aren't part of the past. This is part of my new, post-Felix world. And maybe he is still part of that world, because he is still part of me, and at the same time he is part of the earth and the soil and the sea and the sky and the air and the water and the waves and the droplets and the leaves and the plants and the trees and the grasses and the worms and the birds and the animals and the fish.

12 May

Last night I had another meltdown. I was lying in bed in the dark, thinking about you, when I suddenly became overwhelmed by a tsunami of grief. I now understand what the phrase 'wailing and gnashing of teeth' actually means. It was like being sick: great involuntary waves of groans and wails followed by panting, heavy breathing, all out of control. Eventually it subsided but it was horrifying to experience, and yet at the same time, it felt so appropriate – what has happened is horrific.

Your death is so recent and yet life is bizarrely back to normal – except it isn't, of course. At the beginning we were buoyed along by the shock, the adrenalin; we were simply surviving like corks bobbing along on the surface of a fast-flowing river in a storm. Now the intense weather has stopped and the river is flowing more calmly but I am just starting to realise the true enormity of your loss. I gave birth to you, you were a tiny seed inside me, you grew in my body, you were born, I fed you, I nurtured you, and now you're gone.

I've always felt so afraid of death, but now you have gone I don't feel so afraid any more. In a way I am looking forward to it. Maybe I might be with you again. And yet I have to live, especially for Lucian. I'm sure I can survive, but can I live?

It was January 2010, an ordinary weekday night, and we were in bed. The boys had been tucked up for a couple of hours already. Their rooms adjoined each other and were just across the corridor from ours. I was drifting into sleep when I felt something on my arm. It was Lucian, then aged ten.

'It's Felix! He's fallen out of bed!'

I leapt out of bed and rushed into Felix's room, where he was lying on the floor, twitching. I felt terrified. I put my hand on his shoulder but he didn't seem to notice. I couldn't comprehend what was going on, though somewhere deep inside me, I think I knew. He continued to lie there, jerking. I knelt beside him, soothing him and gently holding his shoulders. Gradually the movement stopped, but we could see he was unconscious. Alex called an ambulance. The paramedics arrived and carried Felix out of the house. Alex went with him to the hospital and I stayed at home with Lucian.

Lying in bed it was hard to sleep. My worst nightmare was coming true. My epilepsy was coming back to haunt me: I was sure Felix had had an epileptic seizure. What did this mean for him? Was this a one-off or was it the start of something? I felt a mixture of anxiety, fear and sadness, and also a sense of the cruelty of life. I felt Felix was being kicked when he was down; life was already tough for him because of the bullying.

The next morning, I drove to the hospital and went to the children's ward as quickly as I could. I got there to find Felix sitting up in bed. 'Everyone here is so kind,' he said. I hugged him and held him close. My dear, darling son.

The doctors said it probably was a seizure, especially given the family history. But they said it could just be an isolated incident, and he might never have any more. However, in the following months he had five more seizures, all of which started while he was asleep. He was put on medication and they stopped. After a couple of years, he decided to try coming off the medication, but the seizures returned. He went back on the medication but they continued, and he started to have seizures while he was awake as well as while he was asleep. His seizures were never properly controlled again.

13 May

I still cannot believe your life has been cut short by epilepsy. I had heard of SUDEP but never dreamed it might happen to you, partly because I have lived with epilepsy for thirty years and have become used to it, familiar with it, unfazed by the loss of consciousness it entails, never worrying that I might never wake up.

You were so stoical about it. It was part of your calm, accepting nature, your lack of ego, your beautiful gentleness that never assumed you had any importance. I remember when you got into the grammar school, you assumed there had been a mistake. And you thought if it wasn't a mistake, you must have had the lowest points of all the candidates and just scraped through.

You accepted your epilepsy; you didn't rail against it. And yet you really suffered. After a seizure, you were bruised and battered. You felt absolutely terrible for at least a day. I remember that time you went on a drama weekend with your friends at the youth theatre. You all stayed in a hostel on Dartmoor, by the River Dart at Dartmeet. I dropped you off on the Friday night and you were excited about being there, with a group of people who accepted and liked you. You loved being part of that supportive group, working together on your play, and were growing in confidence. But on the Saturday morning I had a phone call to tell me that you had had a seizure that morning. I came to collect you and I sensed the concern and embarrassment of the people there, especially the teenagers. You were on your own in the dormitory, waiting for me, and I hugged you as though my life depended on it. I asked if you wanted to stay on for the rest of the weekend and you said no. I was sad about that because I wanted you to experience that weekend. But I also totally understood. You were feeling so rough, and you didn't want to have to deal with other people's reactions on top of that. And you couldn't help feeling ashamed.

I am back in Felix's room, trying to sort out his stuff. I've been dreading tackling his clothes again but decide to bite the bullet. I keep a lot of things, among them his school ties and blazer, though why I'm keeping these I don't really know, as school wasn't exactly his favourite place. The laundry basket is overflowing. As I put his clothes out to dry on the line, I feel so sad. This is the last time I will do this for him, but I still want to parent him. I can't bear the thought of not doing his washing any more.

Later I bring the clothes in. Kate has suggested I make something out of them and I have mentioned this to my friend Ellie. She told me her friend who was widowed had a quilt made out of her husband's clothes. I think I'd like to do this. It would be such a comfort to have on our bed.

Daybreak

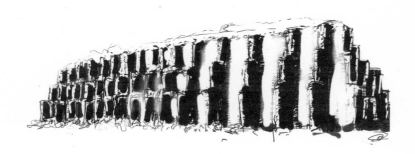

15 May

Do you remember my sunrise custom on the anniversary of Grandma's death? Getting up at dawn and heading up to the old Second World War firing range near Rippon Tor to watch the sun come up over the sea? Well, this year of course the ritual was for you as well.

I felt terrible when the alarm went – I'd slept really badly – but I hauled myself out of bed, made a flask and set off. It was light but the sun wasn't yet up; it was that strange, rather lifeless light, when night is not yet over but the day has not yet begun. As I got out of the car, I saw the moon, still clear and high in the sky, and I was hit by a wall of trills from the birds, a unified sound of singing. It was so thick and loud it was impossible to make out the individual songs. As I walked along towards the firing range, I looked down towards Newton Abbot and the sea. Mist clung to the folds of the Teign Valley and it was all shades of grey and pink.

I climbed up the massive old butt and sat at the top, looking over to where the sky was starting to take on a rosy glow. I saw a crinkle of gold on the horizon and I could see the sun was starting to break through some low-slung clouds. Lines of gold seeped along the edge of the clouds and the sky was molten pink, and it was a process of seconds as a huge smudge of sun burst forth and flooded the sky around it with light.

And all the time this was happening, a pair of stonechats were keeping me company in a nearby gorse bush, hopping around with a constant stream of chatter. I sat there for about forty minutes and they gradually forgot I was there. I watched as the little birds became increasingly bathed in sunlight, their orange plumage glowing.

As I sat watching the sun, I thought about its omnipotence and its inevitability, rising and setting every day with nothing to stop it. I thought about you and Grandma. I'd like to think you and she are somehow present in the sun, that I'm making contact with you by watching the sun in this intimate, solitary way.

A cuckoo was singing its heart out as I walked back to the car, an incessant and repetitive noise.

I am thinking about going back to work. It's been three months now. Maybe it would help, if only as a distraction, but I do feel ambivalent about it — I worry about my ability to concentrate, and the emotional nature of the work.

I've been wondering what I need to say to my colleagues about what has happened. I've somehow got to convey the enormity of this change in my life. I now know that if you haven't experienced the death of a child, it is very hard to understand what the horror feels like, and the impact it has. I have to try, to give them and me the best chance of making it work. A good way of describing it might be to say it's the mental and emotional equivalent of being hit by a lorry. If I'd been hit by a lorry, I'd probably be off for a year, the injuries would be so great – the same, maybe, if I had cancer. My brainpower has also been considerably reduced, and my concentration impaired, rather like the 'baby brain' I remember experiencing as a new mother. I now have a low tolerance for bad news, especially heart-wrenching stuff, which could be tricky as I work as a local news journalist.

I meet a couple of dear colleagues, James and Emma, in a local pub. Apparently, I'm not actually allowed in the BBC building if I'm on a sick note (the doctor has signed me off work). They are really supportive. We decide I'll get a 'fit to work' note specifying what I can and can't do. I will be treated as an 'extra' and not put on the rota, and I'm going to try two days a week, starting next week. I want to give it a go; maybe it could help. I hope it's doable.

Alex and I decide to hike to Ryder's Hill, the highest part of southern Dartmoor. He tells me it's the last long walk he did with Felix. Lucian was there too and both boys complained. I feel a strong urge to follow in their footsteps, to make a kind of pilgrimage. We set out on a beautiful, sunny day with scudding clouds. We ascend slowly and steadily through the quite featureless landscape. Walking together is good. It does not require talking or communication, but we are doing something that creates a feeling of closeness. Felix's death has thrown us into private, separate emotional worlds. We cannot seem to comfort each other, but walking together is quietly helpful.

This part of the moor is devoid of tors and as we climb the wind gets stronger. We skirt around the little valley of the River Mardle, where the landscape feels a bit like the African savannah. It is dotted with small, lollipop-like hawthorns that remind me of baobab trees. We pass a cairn and I add a stone for Felix. It gets boggy, and continues to be boggy even as we get higher – it's that contrary Dartmoor thing of bogs being on the tops and sides of hills, where in theory they shouldn't be. We pass swathes of white fluff – areas of bog cotton like little lambs' tails. Every so often we see patches of ground dotted with tiny, intense-blue flowers, like drops of indigo paint fallen off a passing artist's brush. We later discover they are called heath milkwort. The views get better and better, and by the time we reach the top we can see 360 degrees all around: over to Red Lake with its conical hill, to Buckfast Abbey with its grey-and-yellow tower, and down to the sea off the South Hams coast. It feels good to be out retracing Felix's steps on a walk I haven't done before; perhaps I am making a new tradition? I'm looking for new places to create the new Felix in the absence of the old one, places where we think about him and remember him unencumbered by specific memories.

On the way back, I swim in the Dart in a vast pool by Holne Weir. It is drenched in sunlight and the water is dark and black, after all the recent rain. It feels warm and comforting, though the current is strong.

★

When Felix was sixteen, he had his first and, as it turned out, his only girlfriend, in what ended up being a rather formative summer. He met her on National Citizen Service, which is a free programme for sixteen- to seventeen-year-olds, aimed at getting them volunteering and learning about social responsibility. I dropped him off at a youth club in Newton Abbot on the first day, a little worried about how he would cope with being thrown into a new group of people, especially given his experiences of being bullied at school. I was amazed when I collected him. As he walked out, there was lots of joshing and joking, and shouts of 'Bye, Felix! See you tomorrow!' In the car, he was beaming and animated, chatting about what they'd been doing and the people he'd met. Soon the group was off on a residential where they stayed in North Devon and did outdoor activities like kayaking and surfing. On their return, they spent another couple of weeks together volunteering, gardening at a local centre for young people with disabilities.

I was delighted to find out he had a girlfriend, although we never got to know her as the whole thing turned out to be rather short-lived. The only time we saw them together was when we took her and Felix to an awards ceremony for all the participants. Neither of them said much and the whole thing was a little awkward, but they did hold hands. Sometime afterwards, I saw a photo of them together on the course and I could not believe the animation on his face. He was virtually unrecognisable. He looked really happy. She lived in Plymouth, a little way away, and chucked him a month or so later – he didn't seem that upset. The point was that in this experience, he had fitted in, he had belonged, he had been accepted.

After he died, I found an envelope full of small, hand-written cards, some signed, others anonymous, from members of the group:

'Felix you're so awesome!'

'Hi, your funny. Skyrim sucks. Joking.'

'Felix. You were one of the first people I got to know in the induction session, and thank you for being so friendly. Every time I have spoken to you you've been hilariously witty.'

'Felix. Great to be around and great at surfing.'

'You have good taste in books.'

'Very intellectual and sociable person who is always willing to help out in team situations.'

21 May

Oh darling, it's been a dreary few days. Yesterday it rained ALL day and I stayed in doing very little and eating too much. Today I felt I should make an effort to do something and so went and joined the regular swim over in Torquay even though the weather was still awful. On the journey over there a thick mist shrouded everything. It struck me this is rather like my life at the moment. I can't see ahead at all, only what is immediately in front of me, a grey nothingness enveloping everything.

However, the swim was lovely. It was still overcast but the tide was high, the water was pine green and with a wonderful, tactile viscosity. We swam alongside Corbyn Head, its orange sandstone a contrast to the jade water. It felt warm – in fact the air is quite humid today; things are warming up in spite of the rain. It felt good to launch myself into the sea. The water was comforting; it held me as I moved about, weightless and in the moment.

I felt angry driving back, furious that you've been deprived of your future, that your life has been cut short. I don't know what to do with this anger. I know it's pointless. The only person it affects is me, but I guess I have to feel that anger, to allow it to burn out. It feels like a hard splinter of glass embedded deep in my being, sapping me of humour and optimism. It is all so unjust, and yet no one ever said life was fair – we all know it isn't. I guess that until this point, life has been a lot fairer for me than it has been for other people. Now the balance has slipped the other way. Of course, it's much worse for you than for me: you have lost your life.

I do a lot of thinking and feeling in the car. It's a little box where I can release things in a neutral, mechanical, private space. It's a little gap in time and place, for manageable bursts of emotion, when I am alone and no one can see me, but I am also almost separate from myself. I am driving, I am moving, I am like another being in my metal shell.

Another thing I started thinking about on this particular journey was something another bereaved parent said to me. 'The realisation that you have changed as a person takes a while to sink in.' What did he mean? Have I changed as a person? I don't know. Certainly, what has happened – although I don't know if this is permanent – is a hardening against the world, an awful sense of anger and bitterness, a chip of glass inside my heart that wants to destroy my optimism, my hope, my joie de vivre.

I wake up to the news that twenty-two people, including many children, have been killed in a suicide bombing at a pop concert in Manchester. I feel physically sick, disgusted by the world – this is just too much to bear. There is too much pain. I've been thinking about emotional pain and realising that it is not going to go away, unlike a physical pain, which usually will eventually lessen and then disappear. This is not going to happen with Felix's death. That is what I find so challenging, so unbearable: how am I ever going to learn to deal with it? A friend said it might become 'familiar', which is a way of saying I will get used to it. Yet a part of me is resistant to learning to live with the pain because that involves accepting that he has died, which I can't do at the moment.

Felix's room is still full of boxes. I find this distressing. I want to get the stuff sorted out and for his room to be calm and ordered, but sorting his stuff is something I can't simply get on and do. It's too emotionally wearing. I decide to tackle one box and find various notebooks and schoolwork. I see his handwriting. I find a diary from when he was nine, including some stuff written when Alex and I were away, finishing 'MUMMY AND DADDY ARE HOME!' And then another entry describing his birthday with 'two cakes' as something of great note – all in his young, unsteady hand. I feel wobbly and tearful, and an increasing sense of desperation at the impossibility of escaping the reality of his death. It feels like a form of torture – there is just no getting away from it. In the past, when things have gone wrong, there has always been the feeling that things will get better; whatever the problem was, it was solvable or would cease to be important. This is not solvable. The thought of going ahead with this constant, indescribable pain makes me feel trapped and hopeless.

Alex and I drive up to the moor for a walk. In the car I ask him, 'Do you feel optimistic about the future?' And of course, he points out all there is to be glad and happy about, which is true, but at the moment the pain feels like the only reality. I don't really want to hear about all the good things; they just feel like a total irrelevance, and even a bit of an insult.

The next morning, I wake at 5 a.m. with the dawn chorus. I'm assailed by another flood of weeping, great intakes of breaths and sobs. Usually, I feel a bit better afterwards, but not today. I think the disbelief at Felix's death has melted away and there is no escaping its bold, ugly, massive reality.

We get emails confirming the refund of his university fees and accommodation costs. We decide to give some of the money to the theatre projects he was involved in.

23 May

I think about you all the time. I think about your babyhood, your childhood, your young life, your essence, the collection of molecules that made up FELIX. You dominate my thoughts, yet I cannot reach you. It's still inconceivable you're not here.

It's been getting warmer the last few days. I'm lying in bed with the window wide open, there's a cacophony of birds tweeting in the trees and you're not here. It's Lucian's birthday today and you're not here to celebrate with us. There's a dog barking, a car going by, all these sounds are reminders of life ongoing, but you no longer have life and breath.

Yesterday I was fragile all day, on a knife edge. I felt a sense of anxiety, of underlying unsteadiness. I immersed myself in domestic tasks — changing the beds, making Lucian's birthday cake, cooking dinner, sorting the laundry — before heading out to your lagoon with Anna and Yaara.

The Green Hill

On our arrival the water was sparkling and delicious. We sat down on the huge, sloping rock beside it and admired the turquoise pool. We got in and swam over to the other side, and explored some of the channels and gullies. We laid boulders for you. All the time I was feeling quite tense; I didn't really want to talk, because I felt I would lose control of my emotions at any point. Eventually I did, in the car coming back: I had a good sob — it was a pure release of tension.

Oh darling, it just seems to be getting more and more difficult. I'm going to have to be superhuman to get through this.

Summer camp

3 June

Yesterday felt strangely normal. I didn't feel tearful once. It almost felt as though nothing had happened, that you hadn't died. It's a sense of unreality similar to the first days after you died. I'm going around thinking, How am I functioning, laughing, joking, when this appalling thing has happened?

I went back to the Green Hill yesterday and as I drove through the lanes, I saw the valerians and foxgloves were out in the hedges and banks in a riot of pink. I love this time of year; these flowers of early summer signify sun and warmth and long days ahead. There were lots of the less common dark-red valerians, which I prefer to the bland, paler ones. The foxgloves were striking, shocking-pink spikes leaning out into the roads. I've noticed the sequence of flowers since your death. First primroses and cowslips, then bluebells, now valerians and foxgloves. The burial ground looked beautiful. It has transformed in the last two weeks. Suddenly it's full of waist-high grasses, swaying gently in the breeze. The sextons mow around the graves, so each one stands out, topped with silvery-green grasses, delicate and ethereal. The river was full below, with the wind making ripples on it. I left you one of Grandma's roses. It's called Rosa Mundi, a gorgeous-smelling pink rose with a red stripe through it. Grandma loved her roses. She had another striped one, Tricolore de Flandre, and two dark-pink ones called Prospero and Othello. However, she wasn't so keen on an old one that rambled up the apple tree that she described as 'hideous knicker-pink'.

I stood there in very strong winds by your grave, looking down to the estuary, and thought of your body decaying down below. For the first time, I started to think of it as a collection of flesh and bones — not you. Before I've always felt it's you, your body down there. But this time it felt less personal. I felt the idea of your body had less potency, and I tried to think of your 'spirit' or 'essence' floating around who knows where. That didn't give me great comfort. It's not a concept that has any great resonance for me. I think of you more as a feeling, an emotion inside me. To think that is all you are now is very hard.

Your headstone is still not in place. There's still a space where it should be. This is making me angry.

Alex and I are heading down to East Prawle to camp with friends. The village is the most southerly in Devon and has various campsites in various farmers' fields with varying states of facilities, none of which is very sophisticated. It's a bit of a cult place, especially because it has a pub called The Pigs Nose that is run by a chap who used to be in the music industry. He puts on all sorts of live music. In the past, acts including Blur and Paul Young have played there, and there's always someone interesting and often quite famous coming up. The pub itself is a 'proper' pub: it's tatty inside with worn furniture and baskets of knitting lying around for you to do if you feel like it. Outside a sign reads: 'Free wine gums and snuff. Stress therapy with barmaids.'

We've had a few happy trips there over the years. There was one when I went with my friend Trixie and her two boys, Felix and Rufus. My Felix and Lucian were about thirteen and ten; her boys ten and seven. The weather was atrocious, with torrential rain. We sought refuge in the pub, where we had fish and chips before braving the elements to head back to our tents for the night. The boys were dry and warm in their pop-up tent from Lidl, but about an hour after I turned in, an enormous cascade of water came pouring in above my head. It was a long night. Later, I discovered that a small scrap of canvas I had been puzzled by when pitching was actually supposed to go on top of the tent, where there was a hole. It was possibly the shortest camping trip ever: we were back home in less than twenty-four hours.

Alex and I get to the village in the early afternoon and head for the coast path. We see a yellowhammer, with its bright-yellow head, perched on a telephone line. All the vetches are out: purple vetch, with its tendrils clambering over the hedges, and the bright-yellow kidney vetch, clustering on the ground. There is also orange-and-yellow bird's-foot trefoil, which we call 'eggs and bacon'. We walk along to Ivy Cove, past the cottages where my dad stayed with his brother and grandparents in the 1930s. Back then, fishermen made extra money by taking paying guests, and Dad and his brother Barry, accompanied by their grandparents, stayed with a family called the Logans. One of their descendants, Bill Logan, still lives in the end cottage, tending his veg plot, which teeters over the cliffs. His must be just about the only coastal home on the South Hams that isn't a holiday home. Dad and Barry spent their days going out with the fishermen – the small cove had its own fleet back then – and playing on the beach, swimming and diving. I have a tiny photo album of little black-and-white photos that were taken by their grandmother with her box Brownie camera: my dad standing proudly with a mackerel; Barry wielding a butterfly net in one hand and a rabbit in the other, with the caption 'A double catch'; them both diving off the rock platforms that line the cove. A favourite activity was to hide under the tarpaulins that covered the boats and shoot the rats that swarmed all over the place, as everyone in the cottages above the beach used to chuck their rubbish over the cliff.

Now the cove has no boats, though the rusted old winch remains as a sign of the beach's past, and there are various metal rings welded into the rocks where boats would be moored. We sit on the shingle and look out over the blue, flat sea, clear and calm. I swim, and head off east, exploring a maze of pools and channels formed by the raised beach, a particular feature of this part of Devon. The raised beach, or wave-cut bench, was formed towards the end of the last ice age, around 10,000 years ago, when sea levels dropped. The rocks that I'm swimming among are Lower Devonian schist, probably about 400 million years old and the oldest in Devon. I move slowly through the water, admiring the light twinkling on the pale shingle below and the kelp garden swaying gently as I pass through. I think of my dad here eighty years ago and my heart aches at the thought of him, his childhood, his great age and his long life, and of his grandson, Felix, dead at twenty.

For Dad, Felix's death brought back traumatic memories. When I broke the news to him down the phone, he cried uncontrollably. Barry had been killed aged twenty-three, in the last few months of the war, after being the first British soldier to cross the Rhine. Now I really understand the impact that must have had on them, a small family, like us, with two boys. Little did they know on that holiday in Devon, in 1938, that seven years later Barry would be dead.

Alex and I arrive back at the campsite to find our friends have arrived. We settle down for pre-pub drinks, sitting in our camping chairs, looking out to sea. A drunken evening ensues, with much rowdy behaviour in the pub, followed by the inevitable tripping over the guy rope on the way back in the dark. It was just what we needed, to hang out with friends for a few hours, having a laugh, a temporary sense of normality.

Driving back, the high is followed by a low. I feel tearful in the car, and we talk about whether Felix might still exist. Alex says he feels he is in the earth, part of the earth, and at peace. That is comforting in a way, but it feels impersonal. That's what gets me. The idea of his identity gone. That Felix is no longer an entity, a person with his place in the world: that is really hard. And yet if he is in the earth, now part of something bigger, that must be true of all of us, whether we are alive or dead.

A few days later, Alex and I head up onto the moor to

walk near Widecombe. When we leave Ashburton, it is raining but clear, but as we get higher, we move up into dense fog, which blankets everything in grey wetness. We walk to a hamlet called Heathercombe through a cleared larch plantation, as rain falls and swathes of mist move along the skyline. The larch was brutally felled due to *Phytophthora ramorum* disease; it feels sad and laid to waste. Heathercombe has two ancient, thatched, granite Dartmoor longhouses, where we had a cream tea once. I think the boys were probably with us; it was one of those open garden events.

As a family we have always walked. We started taking the children when they were very young. I remember when we'd just moved to Devon and were living in Exeter. Felix was three and I was pregnant with Lucian. We decided to go and explore Dartmoor, which we didn't know at all at the time. We headed to Chagford, on the northern edge of the moor, a charming town with a picturesque square including a traditional ironmonger that sold everything. From there we drove up to a car park high on the tops, intending to have a walk. It was one of those days when the wind is so strong it could blow you sideways, and opening the car doors to get out was a challenge in itself. We got Felix out, and he was all wrapped up, but he just stood in the car park and refused to move.

'Too wind!' he cried.

And that was the end of that walk. I remember another one, tough and wet, when he was probably about seven, near Scorriton. We had climbed up an old track called Sandy Way that leads up to Holne Moor. We were all clad in waterproofs, which we needed because it was one of those days when you have to put your head down against the driving rain. The track uphill was stony and slippery, and it was a relief to get to the top and then start going back down in a circle to the village. The last bit of path was like a dark tunnel, sheltered by trees, and I still have a vision of Felix and Lucian running ahead, splashing in the puddles, their yellow wellies like bright lights flickering in the gloom.

We also took the boys on lots of walks along the coast path. There's a bit that is really good for children between Thurlestone and Hope Cove. You walk along the top of the cliffs, with stunning views out to sea, and there are hardly any major inclines. There are also several points where they can run ahead safely as the path is some distance from the edge. On one occasion this is what they did – they disappeared from view, only to ambush us a few hundred yards ahead, jumping out from behind a bush, crying 'Suicide bombers!' This was amusing but also rather disturbing. I remember thinking, yes, they are definitely twenty-first-century boys; suicide bombing was not a concept I was familiar with when I was a child.

5 June

I want oblivion. I want an escape from this inescapable reality. I've woken up this morning and it's heavy rain again, and the best thing would be if I could just go back to sleep and be unaware. But I can't.

Yesterday afternoon I started to get that feeling of pointlessness again, and started looking through all my photos on the computer in the hope of finding a picture of you that I haven't seen recently.

I found a lovely one of you lying on the beach reading a book, at Kynance Cove down on the Lizard in Cornwall, looking relaxed and handsome. You were holding your book above your head, turning to smile at the photographer (me) and squinting in the sun. It broke my heart.

Earlier I was in Torquay to pick Lucian up from school and I drove past the clinic at the hospital where I used to take you to see that lovely Italian paediatrician about your epilepsy. It made me very sad. Thinking of all the time we spent trying to get your epilepsy under control. It now all feels such a waste. Dad came home and he was also feeling the blues. There was nothing on TV and we played Scrabble. I complained constantly as I had nothing but vowels.

Later, as I was getting ready for bed, I remembered that earlier on in the day I had bought a loaf of bread. It was the usual full-size loaf. Suddenly I thought, Why did I buy that? A small loaf would be perfectly big enough for us now.

Alex and I have a huge row. It starts over photos. I'm sorting through them, looking for pictures of Felix to frame, to have around the house. Alex tells me he is worried Lucian will be jealous if there are lots of photos of Felix. I disagree, and in any case I can see Lucian every day, whereas I will never see Felix again. Then Alex asks me, somewhat aggressively, how I 'feel', and then it descends into a row about who feels the grief more, or whose grief is worse. What I find challenging is his apparent lack of emotion. He appears to be behaving as normal, as though Felix hasn't died. Of course, I know he's in agony inside, but there is no obvious sign of it. I can't keep my emotions hidden in the same way. I was crying yesterday and he came and asked me, 'What's the matter?' That infuriated me. *Well, what the bloody hell do you think is the matter? Our beloved son has died!*

Another day, Alex produces a small bunch of grasses that he ties together and arranges in a small vase. He tells me he visited Felix's grave a few days earlier and picked them. I'm shocked. He never told me he was going. He didn't ask me to come. Of course, it is up to him what he does and there is no need to confer with me. But it makes me sad that he doesn't share his grief. Rightly or wrongly, I feel excluded. To him, I think sharing means a doubling of the pain, and he's also very private. We are so different emotionally – we always have been. He is an introvert who keeps his feelings inside. I am the opposite; I need to express what's going on. Somehow, we have to learn to get through this without causing each other any more pain.

8 June

Darling, I'm sitting here drinking tea out of my treasured Poldark mug – the one you gave me. I remember that occasion so well. We were in Cadgwith, that picturesque fishing village in Cornwall, with its brightly coloured day boats dominating the small beach. We were buying ice creams at the gift shop. Later you handed me a paper bag and in it was the mug, with a picture of Aidan Turner naked from the waist up, brandishing a scythe. It was inscribed 'Ross Poldark's Grass Cutting Service'. I laughed my head off and was so touched that you thought of buying it for me. You said that initially you thought you'd save it for my birthday but you were so keen to see my reaction you gave it to me there and then.

Yesterday I was looking through your stuff again. I opened up your wallet and looked at the receipts. I felt I was intruding but I also had that insatiable desire to know everything about you, a desperate longing to know and possess everything of you. I particularly feel like this about the last months of your life when I wasn't there; I'm just trying to make sense of it all. I found lots of receipts for fizzy drinks and junk food from Asda. I still feel upset about that — you seeking comfort in junk food, which upset me when you were alive and upsets me still. And it contrasts with the pictures in my mind of you as young and innocent and perfect as a child, before the inevitable (I suppose) corruption of later years. I want to remember you as perfect, unblemished, but that is not possible. You were tarnished, like all of us, and in fact you had a greater cross to bear than many young people, so it's not surprising you sought comfort. Anyway, who am I to talk about comfort-eating? I suppose your children reflect your failings back at you.

Back to work

10 June

Oh Felix, I miss you so much. I miss your smile, I miss your quiet presence, I miss your hugs, I miss the way you always noticed if I glammed up to go out and said, 'You look nice!'

You weren't perfect, of course. None of us is. You were irritating sometimes, especially last year, when you were at home for most of the year before starting at Leicester afresh. You lay around a lot and didn't do very much. I remember you getting sacked from that job at the River Dart Country Park for failing to turn up to work one too many times. And that came on top of being sacked from a call centre, after you had a seizure while at work. I still feel full of rage at the injustice of that. It was discrimination but you didn't want to make a fuss. You were so lost at that time, not knowing where your interests really lay, not having friends, stuck at home. It was all part of the struggles you had in your teen years, in which I think the epilepsy played a significant part. You were already quite shy and lacking in confidence, and the epilepsy made that so much worse. But you never complained.

I've been continuing to go through all your stuff. So many things just bring me up short. Today I found your sixth-form work, and an exercise book from when you were about nine. There's a hard and indestructible knot of pain deep inside me and I can't imagine it ever going away.

Lucian and I chatted in the car yesterday about his plans. He told me he wanted to make a positive difference in whatever he does. He mentioned you and the fact you were just starting out and had been robbed of the chance to do that. And the importance of grabbing life with both hands as you never know when it will end.

I can't help feeling that your life was doomed. It was a battle to survive when you were born and there were many periods when you struggled: being bullied at primary school and at secondary (mercifully I've forgotten the full details); your struggle to make friends; your struggle with epilepsy. Life was undeniably challenging and it makes me so sad to think about that. I know there were happy times but I can't seem to focus on those at the moment; I just think about the difficulties you had and then you DIED, just as they were starting to fade into the background. This just doesn't fit with the narrative we're born to expect, where we pass through childhood and adolescence, go out into the world and make a life. It may be an unrealistic narrative, but we're all led to believe in the fairy tale.

My friend Catherine and I meet in Teignmouth to swim at the Parson and Clerk. These are rock formations in the red cliffs by Parsons Tunnel, through which Brunel's famous railway goes. The Parson protrudes from the end of the cliffs, with an archway through which you can swim. The Clerk is a small stack island (getting smaller every year) just off the shore. This coastline, with its terracotta cliffs, was created millions of years ago, when the area was a hot desert plain. The cliffs, being so old, feel, to me, like a graphic embodiment of time, and our place in it, something I have been thinking about so much since Felix died.

Catherine and I walk along the railway wall towards the northern end of the beach, which is where the rail line disappears into the tunnel. She naturally asks how I am, and I come out with a phrase that keeps rebounding around my head at the moment: 'clinging to the wreckage'. I feel as though I'm hanging on by my fingernails to what I have left.

When, earlier, I'd looked at the webcam for Teignmouth, the water was looking flat calm, and perfect for a swim through the arch. I've had a couple of goes at this before but the sea has always been too rough to get through. However, in reality, when we get there today the sea is quite steely and choppy. The weather is all over the place – there are looming grey clouds and then bursts of sunshine.

Trains rumble by on the line behind us as we get changed. We wade into the water and then launch off into the chop. We are buffeted by the waves as we bounce along past the cliffs on our left, admiring their astonishingly bright red colour and their tufty green vegetation like unruly clumps of hair. We see a smart little oystercatcher, startling in black and white, standing sentinel on a rock.

We look up and see gulls in their nests in niches in the cliff above us. We pass the Clerk and approach the arch, magnificent and grand with its dramatic horizontal stripes of rock. We are unceremoniously bounced and tossed towards it by the wind and waves, and as we are swept through, we look up at its might overhead, and back through to the small phallic Clerk, framed by the opening. Once we are through to the other side, it's like being in another place entirely. It is sheltered, and the sea is calm and a beautiful petrol-blue against the brick-red cliffs. We swim languidly, enjoying the flat water, and are heading towards a large cave when suddenly we catch sight of a big seal, about 200 yards away. That's way too close in my book.

I have a bit of a history with seals. I remember the first time I encountered one in the water. I was with Anna at Hope Cove. We were swimming quite far into the bay at Inner Hope, aiming for a little island in the middle. I thought I saw something dark out of the corner of my eye but dismissed it. Then I felt something touch my leg – and I dismissed that too. Then, a couple of minutes later, a large, smooth head with huge, soulful eyes popped up right in front of us. My first thought was, *Oh, wow, how wonderful to be so close to such a beautiful creature in its native habitat.* But this quickly changed to panic when it leaned its head back, snorted through its very big nostrils and sank back into the sea, from where it was of course invisible and able to bump us without prior warning.

Ever since, I have given seals a wide berth, so Catherine and I turn tail and head back through the arch, and we find it is really hard going. Carelessly, we had not been paying attention when swimming out, and only now we realise that we were carried most of the way to the arch with little effort on our part. Now, we find heading back against the wind and current is really tough. Every time we make a stroke forward, we get pushed back by big waves. At one point I feel as though we aren't making any progress at all, but try not to worry. Then, I find myself in a moment of not caring what happens. I indulge the feeling for a short while, then snap out of it and try to think what to do. We decide to give up trying to make a straight line back to the shore, and instead head for a nearby rock where we can get out and have a rest. We sit there for a while and then get back in; re-energised, we push back to the shore through the unfriendly swell.

It's a relief to get back on dry land. We talk about what's just happened. We were frightened, we got pretty cold, but at least we were out there, connecting with the elements, living. For me, at a very basic level, it was about distracting myself from the enormity of what has happened, putting myself at the mercy of the elements, and of nature, red in tooth and claw. To be perfectly honest, I didn't care about putting myself in danger. I want to live, really live, and I don't mind if I die in the process.

I go to see the doctor to discuss going back to work. We agree I'll start with two mornings a week. Just thinking about going back to work makes me anxious. It's not so much the work itself, though that is daunting. It's the thought of seeing everyone; everyone's sympathy. It's overwhelming. I decide to write a letter to everyone, to try to make it easier. This is what I write:

Hi everyone,

Thank you so much for your lovely messages of support over my son Felix's death. Everyone's kindness has meant a great deal.

I thought it would be a good idea to write to you just to explain what happened, and also a few thoughts on coming back to work and how that should be handled.

Felix was twenty and, as some of you might know, had epilepsy. It had proved quite difficult to get under control but he'd started at university in Leicester, where he was having a happy time making friends and getting involved in drama. Back in March, I had some leave to use up so went up to Leicester to see him in a show – The Producers. *He never turned up at our meeting place, and to cut a long story short, I raised the alarm and he was found dead in his room. The police and the coroner were involved, and as you can imagine it was a very traumatic time.*

Eventually the coroner recorded his death as SUDEP – Sudden Unexpected Death in Epilepsy. It is very little understood. It affects mostly young people between the ages of twenty and forty.

We've created an online memorial to Felix where donations can also be given to SUDEP Action, a small charity that helps people bereaved by epilepsy but also aids research, including compiling a register of SUDEP deaths. You can have a look at the memorial here: http://felix.murdin.muchloved.com/

I'm coming back to work, initially two days a week, and I will be an 'extra', i.e. not on the rota. I'm really looking forward to seeing everyone, but I'm aware that some people might feel a bit nervous about what to say to me. Death is something we all find difficult and if you are lucky enough not to have had a major bereavement then you might worry about saying the wrong thing.

Basically, don't worry. If you want to talk to me about Felix then I'm really happy to talk about it. I've just given the details above because I didn't want to have to keep telling the same story over and over again. Similarly, if you don't mention it, I won't be offended. And if you don't normally talk to me when I come into the office, then don't feel you have to talk to me now!
xxx
Sophie

I find one of Felix's holiday scrapbooks from a family trip to Rome in 2008, when he was ten and Lucian was seven. We took them out of school in early February. The city was beautifully quiet, cold and sunny. We stayed in an apartment near the Spanish Steps, very near Rome's most famous ice cream parlour and the Sicilian church. It was the first time we'd taken the boys on a 'cultural' holiday and they were very excited to be going on an aeroplane, and then getting a taxi and heading into a city packed full of ancient buildings the like of which they had never seen before.

We quickly got used to our neighbourhood, popping down to the supermarket below our flat or around the corner for ice creams, and walking the streets and visiting the tourist spots. In Felix's notebook there are smudgy pencil sketches of lots of the places: the Circus Maximus, with imagined horse-drawn chariots racing round, the front of the Pantheon with its Corinthian columns, and a wonderfully abstract version of the 'Collasseum' with the caption: 'I copied this from a book before I went to Rome.'

Our visit to the Colosseum followed some time spent

wandering around the Forum. We queued at the official ticket office after being stopped by several ticket touts offering us tours. As we got near the front of the queue, I rummaged in my handbag to get my purse, only to find it gone. I'd fallen victim to a distraction and a pickpocket scam – I felt pretty sure that one of the 'touts' was the culprit. All part of the Rome experience, I suppose. The Colosseum was spectacular. We walked round and round the endless levels, imagining the roaring crowds and the gladiators below.

Another of Felix's sketches shows the Campo de' Fiori, Rome's market square, with its scores of colourful stalls. We were fascinated by the food on offer, in particular the puntarelle, a sort of pale-green straggly chicory that we'd never seen before. We took some back to the flat and had it for dinner. Another day we visited the Vatican, in all its magnificent grandeur, and we became regulars at the Villa Medici at the top of the Spanish Steps, with its lovely gardens and café overlooking the city. The boys were particularly keen on the hot chocolate.

Over a decade on, I look back at the photos. Felix and Lucian are standing either side of the famous statue of the wolf with Romulus and Remus suckling underneath. Felix is looking at the statue, while Lucian stares straight at the camera, his coat falling off his shoulders. Another picture shows Felix standing by a plinth with an enormous foot on it and smiling under his thick, blond fringe. Another shows them both with ice creams, faces covered in chocolate, Felix wearing his newly purchased Roma baseball cap.

12 June

I can feel you fading away and it makes me feel so sad. I'm going back to work soon, which I feel anxious about, as it is a sign of 'normality' returning and that sort of feels like drawing a veil over your death. I never want to do that. It's this thing of trying to create the 'new normal' – shaping life ahead with you in it but in a different way from before. I think I will go and see your grave later and I need to do that before I go back to work tomorrow.

It's Father's Day soon. I'm hoping Alex is not going to be too upset. I am thinking back to when you were born and the role Alex played. In the first few months, I remember he spent a lot of time taking you out for walks strapped to his chest in the sling. You were quite a sicky baby and I remember he frequently came back with your vomit embedded into the corduroy grooves of the sling. Later, when you were about two or three, and walking, we would take you down to the park, where you would run around in your little yellow wellies. We'd put you in the toddler swings – the ones with the little frame that holds the child in place – and push you, your laughter echoing and intensifying as you swung higher and higher.

I go to the Green Hill, where everything is crazily bursting into life. The willow arch at the entrance is a riot of fresh, green leaves, the grasses are higher than before and it is hot. Felix's grave looks beautiful, with masses of different grasses growing from it, as well as buttercups and some tiny pink cranesbill flowers. I lie down beside it in a foetal position, my face pushed into the grass. There are larks calling and responding overhead, and occasionally a fly buzzes past. An insect crawls up my arm and, through it all, there is the gentle sound of the breeze brushing through the grasses on his grave. It feels both beautiful and ironic: all that life springing forth and Felix dead below. I cry into the grass. I lie there for quite a while and then hear voices. I stay where I am, hidden by Felix's grave, not wanting to see anyone. Eventually the voices disappear. I turn over and lie on my back. It gets really warm and I have to take off a couple of layers. I am happy just being there with Felix. I have some mother-of-pearl shells I'd gathered at Shell Island, and I place one of the heart-shaped ones on his grave as I leave.

The next morning, I am lying on my bed waiting for my nails to dry before going into work. I'm thinking about what it will be like seeing everyone again. So much has changed since I was last there. I feel very nervous about it.

As I drive into the car park, I immediately start feeling tearful. Physically being here is a shockingly visceral experience, powerfully taking me back to the time before Felix died, when life was normal, when the horror hadn't happened. It is overwhelming, it is like a flashback to the 'before', which brutally emphasises the horror of the 'after'. I am surprised by the intensity of my physical reaction.

I go into the building and straight into the studio, where my friends on the breakfast show are mid-broadcast. The first person I see is James, who is producing, and I immediately burst into tears. Then I go and see Gordon, who's on air, and cry again. The familiarity, the friendliness, the normality of their faces is so out of kilter with my life now, it feels like a lurid contrast. I head for the loo to calm down. I get a coffee and go up to the newsroom, where I am tearful again but I manage to hold it together. Everyone is lovely, and they don't crowd me. A few say they were grateful for the email, which they found helpful. I find a desk and log in, and gradually the initial shock of being back in the workplace recedes and I start to enjoy my return. I'm only there for a few hours, and leave for home after lunch.

It's baking warm and I head to Ladies Pool with Yaara and Anna, where we have the most delicious swim. Ladies Pool is one of our regular haunts in the River Dart, a short walk from New Bridge. It is a large, deep, oval pool above a bubbling cascade. We were swimming there once and a chap sitting nearby told us its name was Ladies Pool. I've often wondered if he just made that up, as a flirtatious conversational gambit. Anyway, as far as we're concerned, that's its official name.

The river is pure balm. The water is gorgeously clear and we swim lazily, chatting. Then, at the end of our swim, we each lay a boulder for Felix on the riverbed. My stone has a white, splodgy heart-shape on it. I hope to find it another time and lay it down it for him again.

15 June

Yesterday Dad and I had a beautiful walk to Avon Dam. I felt the need to be in a large, anonymous, abstract piece of water. We set off through gradually ascending meadows, battling very strong winds that were pushing against us, and passed patches of speedwell, orchids (great excitement) and fading buttercups. As we got higher, we looked back, and the views over to South Devon were stunning. We then emerged onto the moor itself, gloriously bleak with fast-moving clouds and their shadows scudding across the sky. It got boggy, with clumps of bog cotton. Then we caught our first sight of the reservoir, like a little inland sea, with waves created by the strong winds and sun glistening on the water. As we approached, it got bigger, more forbidding. I got in. The water was very clear at the edges, and I was soon into the dark centre, feeling lost in its hugeness.

Again, I felt that closeness to you in the water; it's hard to explain – 'closeness' is probably not the right word. It's more to do with connection. A kind of communication in the water, with my body immersed, feeling part of the earth and the water; of matter itself. It goes back to that famous line from Genesis, as translated in the King James Bible: 'Dust thou art and unto dust shalt thou return.'

Drought

19 June

My darling, we are in the middle of a heatwave. The West Dart was 20 degrees yesterday! And the Dart was 18.9 – warmer than the sea. Outside it is roasting and the streets are full of young lads with their tops off. You should be among them, enjoying yourself in the heat. But you're not. You're not here. I still can't believe that.

I feel as though I am living a double life. There is the external me, the me friends see, the me work sees, the cheerful, friendly me, usually making people laugh, or generally participating, being the life and soul. Then there is the internal me, grieving for you, feeling the desperation of sadness, the constant pain of your loss. It's such a lonely thing. No one can feel it except me. And the me that's feeling it is a different character from the 'Sophie Pierce' of before, who didn't have this inner, extra character – this extra personality, if you like. There was congruency before, between the inner and the outer; now they feel like two different people. Which is me? They are both me.

I went to see your grave earlier. It's so hot today that it's been officially declared the hottest day in June since the heatwave of 1976. I made you a bouquet from the hedgerows of valerian, cow parsley and clover.

Anna and I head for Heybrook Bay, a coastal village near Plymouth that is not posh and gentrified, although houses still cost a bomb there. It feels as though most properties are people's homes and not holiday lets. The water here is very clear as the coastline is very rocky, with little sand, and I often see divers setting off from the beach with underwater photography equipment.

We walk along the coast path towards Wembury. The foxgloves are out, like drunken sailors in the meadows, bending over in the breeze. We also see lots of scabious clinging to the top of the cliff, and a carpet of yellow-and-orange vetch. The path winds down to Wembury Point, where there is a large, flat area just above the beach. This was home, in the 1930s, to Wembury Point Holiday Camp, which had around 200 wooden chalets. A display board by the path shows a black-and-white photo of the Heybrook Bay lido, a tidal pool that was built on the little beach there. Old postcards advertise it, proudly proclaiming its motto: *'Where Sky and Sea are Lido Blue'*. Today you can still see the remains of the lido – its seaward wall is still mostly intact, although the rest of it has gone.

Drought

A short way offshore is the Mewstone, a small island looking like a shark's fin protruding above the water. It is now home only to seals and birds, though it was once 'Plymouth's Alcatraz'. In 1744, according to the National Trust, which now owns it, a local man found guilty of a minor crime was sentenced to stay on the island for seven years. He ended up staying there for the rest of his life, and his daughter, known as Black Joan, remained there, marrying and raising three children on the island. By the early 1800s, another family had moved in. Samuel Wakeham had been due to be transported to Australia, but negotiated to live on the Mewstone instead. He and his wife used to charge curious tourists tuppence to visit the island. The day-trippers had to stand on the mainland beach and wave a white handkerchief to summon him in his boat.

Anna and I head down to the rocky shore, where there are the remains of a slipway and boathouse. The latter makes a perfect changing room. We walk into the water, our feet protected by shoes, and start to swim, our snorkels protruding above the surface. The water gets deeper. We pootle in and around the channels and gullies that make up the enormous reef that stretches out from the shoreline. The underwater world is utterly absorbing. The water is crystal clear, and we swim along above black-and-white-striped rocks and lots of pink seaweed. We notice lots of pieces of pottery in the rock pools. Anna finds a piece of blue-and-white willow-pattern china, and part of a decorated brown teapot spout. Perhaps these items were used by a family camping here eighty years ago? We can imagine a group of people sitting just a few yards from here, admiring the view, perhaps warming up after a swim by drinking tea from a Brown Betty pot. Little did they know the fragments of their lives would be picked up by two women swimming here nearly a century later.

I think back to countless family holidays by the sea. We've never been great campers, but there was one holiday, when the boys were thirteen and ten, that was rather memorable, when we rolled up at Robbie Love's campsite just outside Polzeath, on the North Cornwall coast. We chose Robbie Love's mainly because it was cheap, but also because it was near Porthcothan, a little further down the coast, where we were meeting the extended Pierce family for a week's holiday a few days later. The campsite opened back in the rave days of the late 1980s, and still has rather a party atmosphere as well as being home to seasonal workers every summer. Its website proudly declares: '*Robbie Love's Campsite was established in the summer of 1986 and still retains the charm, character and easy going atmosphere that sets it apart from other campsites. There are no extra charges for cars, awnings, dogs etc, camping in a tent still costs just £12 per person per night.*'

The campsite was in a perfect location near the beach. Luxuries were in short supply. I remember the office, an old Portakabin that was usually unoccupied, with empty drinks bottles and dirty coffee cups lying about. The showers were pretty dreadful, but the field we camped in was stunning, with views over the fields and clifftops. It was the overflow field, so we were a safe distance from the ravers, but I do remember a nearby tepee where there seemed to be quite a bit of dubious activity.

On the first day we headed down to Polzeath to go bodyboarding. The beach was packed and the tide was out. Almost immediately, Felix managed to slash his foot on an exposed mussel shell, so it was off to the lifeguards for first aid. I felt so sorry for him, as he had to spend the rest of the week wearing socks and wellies, because he wasn't allowed to get his foot wet.

A few days later, we met my parents, my three brothers, sister-in-law and three nieces at Porthcothan. We stayed in a big, stone house with Gothic-arched windows just up from the beach, which my parents had rented. It was the thirteenth year we had all holidayed together, having started in 1997 in Daymer Bay. It was a five-minute walk down to the beach, where we spent many happy hours bodyboarding and where the children, particularly, loved a big, sandy pool that appeared at low tide.

We often used to walk south along the coast path to Porth Mear, a shingle beach with a large reef and lots of rock pools. On the way, just on from Porthcothan, is a beautiful, huge, curved wooden seat overlooking the cliffs. I have a lovely photo of the boys and their cousins sitting on it looking out to sea. The seat has a stone plaque on it that reads:

Paul Simon Brewer
aka Paolo . . . Poz . . .
Brewski . . . Brrr –
Lived Life to the Full
6th August 1983
4th March 2010
His Spirit Lives On

I later learned that this young man actually came from our own town, Ashburton. He was working out in Morocco for a surfing company when he died in a road accident. Apparently Porthcothan was where he really got the surfing bug. At the time I felt so sad. Little did I know my own son would later die a sudden unexpected death, too.

3 July

Last night, before I went to sleep, the image of you lying dead in your room came to me again as it frequently does; of your body between your bed and the desk — so distressing. This image comes unbidden into my mind constantly. Although, of course, I never actually saw you like that, I knew your room and so I can't help but imagine it. My mind keeps returning to it, I think because it is so utterly senseless, it is so wrong; it should not have happened. And I think it comes into my mind so frequently because I am your mother, I will always be your mother — and yet I wasn't there.

I wasn't there.

I know, rationally, of course, there was no reason why I should have been there. There's nothing I could have done; this was your time to break free and make your way in the world, independently. But as Grandma used to say to me, 'I'll always be your mother and you'll always be my baby, however old you are.' And as your mother, I feel heartbroken that I wasn't there and couldn't help.

I have started work on your quilt. I spent yesterday afternoon with Milla on the initial preparations. She showed me one her mother had made — a simple patchwork of squares machine-sewn together. It is easy to make, and really beautiful, and so we are going to make yours to the same design. We did various mathematical calculations (getting rather confused, but we got there) to work out how many squares of fabric we will need. After we'd done that, we also talked about how we could beautify your grave, and planned a sequence of flowers to plant there.

Drought

I still can't believe I am talking about your grave. This is real. This is real. This is real. However much I write it, I still can't believe it. And yet I think I am starting to believe it, because the waves of pain that come over me with no warning are getting more intense. They can be prompted at any time. I was playing the piano yesterday and I looked up at your photo in its frame and there you were, the most beautiful boy, and I wept and wept.

Today I started cutting out the fabric for the quilt. First, I ironed all the shirts and pyjamas of yours that I'd washed. Then I made a cardboard template and drew round it on the fabric, making lots of individual squares of material. I spent about three hours on this rather boring work and by the end I had a very sore wrist and shoulder. Darling, I never was cut out for manual labour! And yet I felt deeply comforted by this mundane task. Handling the clothes you wore, making them into something beautiful, transforming them into a memorial of you, is a way of relating to you, of being with you, almost.

I've set up a JustGiving page as we are going to climb Ben Nevis in October in your memory, and to raise money for SUDEP Action. I am so heartened as we've raised nearly a thousand pounds already. I've been looking at the map and have realised there is a loch about a third of the way up that could make a handy swimming challenge, too. It's about half a mile long so I am going to swim that. People's generosity has really cheered me up.

Lucian and I get up early to take the train to Bristol. We're going to a university open day, and of course it takes me back to the trips I did with Felix, to Sussex and Leicester. It is the hottest day of the year so far and we tramp around the halls of residence and lecture theatres getting ever sweatier. It is all new for Lucian, and is an important next stage for him, as it was for Felix. I am excited for him, but Felix casts a shadow.

In the afternoon, we separate to do our own thing. Feeling exhausted, I amble along towards some shops when I notice a church with an A-board outside saying 'Welcome. Please come in. Teas.' So I go in. It turns out to be an Eastern Orthodox church inside a Victorian building. Icons are everywhere, and it is cool and welcoming. The church, which is dedicated to the Nativity of the Mother of God, was founded in 1948 by Polish ex-servicemen and their families. As a lapsed Roman Catholic, I feel drawn to churches, whatever their denomination, and enjoy their sense of quiet and peace. The familiarity is comforting. I particularly love the icons; here they adorn the altar, two-dimensional figures edged in gold. I light a candle for Felix. I want there to be candles burning for him all over the world.

Back home, Alex and I head for a secret stretch of the West Dart that Felix and I discovered last summer. I want to go there because I remember that day very well. Felix was living at home, having given up his law degree. It was actually quite a tense time. He was supposed to be earning money before starting a new degree course later that year. He'd got the sack from his job at the local country park because he failed to turn up one too many times, and he was spending most of his time in his room sleeping or playing on the computer. Relations were rather strained, but I managed to persuade him to come with me to explore part of the West Dart that I was curious about. It was sunny and we parked by Dunnabridge Pound, a Bronze Age stone enclosure, then walked down the rocky path towards the river, with its familiar stepping stones and distinctive clump of pine trees ahead in the distance. My friend Anna calls this area 'the Winnie-the-Pooh place', and we spent a lot of time with the boys here when they were little as there is a sandy beach and shallow water. This time, instead of going downstream as usual, we walked upstream, trespassing through a couple of fields. We found an overgrown set of stepping stones that we'd never seen before, and crossed over into new territory. We walked along boulder-strewn ground and through an ancient gateway into a beautiful pastoral scene with a slow, open stretch of river, where I swam and Felix took photos. It was a quiet, happy day, in which we simply enjoyed being with each other.

I retrace those steps with Alex. It is warm and we lie on the flat, grassy bank in the same spot where I spent time with Felix. This feels helpful. I swim, and the water is so clear and cleansing, like a restorative balm. We walk a little further upstream and find a small plunge pool surrounded by large, mossy boulders with a little cascade. Again, I get in the water and feel its therapeutic powers, finding some temporary relief.

8 July

Yesterday at work I saw someone I haven't seen since before you died. She revealed she'd lost her son when he was four. I think she's the first person I've met who has had a comparable experience. Her loss was many years ago. She said the wound does heal eventually but the scar is always there.

Then I had a text telling me your headstone was finally ready. I was so delighted. But this quickly turned to anger when I had another text, twenty-four hours later, telling me the stonemason had got your dates wrong. He'd put 1977 as your birth year instead of 1997. Unbelievable! And after we've waited so long. I'm furious.

I'm in such a lonely place. This is not something that most people have to deal with. I feel so wounded, so incapacitated by losing you. This week's been tough. Working again, albeit only very part-time, has been a strain. I'm just not used to working, and managing the rest of my life, and grieving for you at the same time. I am realising that grieving is actually work. For example, visiting your grave takes not just time but physical and emotional energy.

Yesterday I went into your room and looked in your chest of drawers. In one drawer were your school ties. They broke my heart. Somehow, they symbolise that growth of you as a person, your learning, your education, all preparing you to make a life that never happened.

Then I looked in my little box where I keep your small, personal things — your wallet, your keys, things like that. I looked at your glasses and I wept.

Launching boats

14 July

Sweetie, it is Bastille Day, Dad's birthday, and it feels so wrong, appallingly wrong, senseless, that you're not here. By rights you should be home from university and loafing about. But, incomprehensibly, you're not. You're gone.

Yesterday we went to the Green Hill to check your headstone, which we'd been told was finally in place. I was so anxious about this, what with all the delays and them getting your dates wrong. I was worried the stone would look awful and that it might be on the wrong grave. But it was there and it was beautiful. Very simple letters carved into a plain piece of slate. What a relief. I didn't realise quite how distressing this issue of the headstone had become. Now it's done, I realise how important it is. It brings a sense of completion and peace to your resting place; your name, your dates are there – you are in a marked grave.

I have done my first full five-day week back at work. It has gone OK but I feel my time with Felix has been squeezed. I need time to mourn, and it is not as easy when you don't have much time. Work takes over my brain, requiring concentration and attention. It takes me away from grieving. Yet it is also a distraction, which is helpful. But now, at the end of the week, I'm feeling emotionally depleted and asking 'Where is Felix?' I'm feeling distanced from him. I need to think about him, talk to him, keep him alive in my mind and in my heart.

Lucian is heading off to London for a few days. I take him to the station, and we stand on the platform at Newton Abbot in the same place I saw Felix off in January. I didn't know it then, but it would be the last time I would ever see him. I feel a deep, physical wave of pain going through me at that memory. We stand together and the train arrives. I hug Lucian and he gets on board. I can't see him because of the reflection in the train window.

I sit down and watch the train pull out and I feel utterly desolate. Desolate at the memory of the last time I ever saw Felix. Desolate that my remaining child is leaving. I wonder, will he come back? I can't help fearing that he won't, which, rationally, I know is unlikely. But fear is so much stronger than reason.

17 July

Last night I was so restless, trying to get to sleep. My mind was full of you, imagining your last few days on earth, what they were like, when I last 'spoke' to you on WhatsApp on the Sunday when you were rehearsing so hard. God, darling, I miss you so much. I feel distraught that you were deprived of your adulthood and only lived for twenty years. I feel so desperately sad that you never found love or made love. There is such a deep sense of sadness about your life that I cannot shift. The fact we named you Felix: it seems so cruel now. Life was hard for you. Struggling to make friends, struggling with the epilepsy, being bullied at school, the weight gain as a result of the medication. It feels dreadful to say it, but you did have a sad life in some ways, in comparison to other youngsters. This makes me feel so miserable and helpless, and yet it helps to write it down, to say it. I wish I could have made things different. I almost feel there was a kind of inevitability about your death. And yet it happened just as you were starting to come out of that dark, tough place. How cruel is that?

It is the wedding of two dear friends, Amanda and Aiden. We arrive at the venue, a beautiful thatched farm in the Devon countryside, and see lots of old friends, including Jeff, who now lives in America and who we haven't seen for about twenty-five years. As soon as I see him, I burst into tears. He is warm and loving and big and bear-like, and it's that kind of feeling of an old connection, back to when we were so much younger, that somehow intensifies the emotion and the enormity of what has happened. Seeing him for the first time since Felix's death, our relationship has to adjust to take in this life-shattering event that has happened in the intervening years, in which he has had two children, moved abroad and made a whole new life.

There are also, of course, guests that we don't know. Chatting over drinks, someone asks me, 'Do you have children?' This is the first time this has happened since Felix died. I think for a moment and then reply: 'Well, I had two but my elder son died earlier this year.' It is dreadful to see her shock, but what else could I say? I explain about SUDEP and of course then I start worrying about her, the fact that I've upset her. No doubt this will not be the only time this happens. I will have to start to learn to deal with these situations.

The wedding ceremony happens outside. I sit with Sean, Felix's godfather, who is playing the piano for the bride's entrance, and turn the pages of the music for him. Sean is Felix's number-one fan and has always been the most brilliant godfather, taking such an interest, being in touch, sending really special presents. It is good to be beside him, to feel his solidarity while attending another rite of passage, a rite of passage that somehow feels heightened by the death of my son.

The next day, Sean, his husband Steve and I head to the Green Hill. It is a windy, changeable day, beautiful in its vigour, the clouds scattering into the distance and the grasses bending in the breeze. I find some purple vetch in the hedgerow and put it on Felix's grave. Sean hugs me and tells me Felix knows I am there. I am not sure. I would like to think that but I don't honestly know.

29 July

Oh my darling, I am in a kind of madness. It feels intolerable. There is nowhere I can go beyond your death. It is the most massive full stop, yet it is not a logical ending like a full stop; it's simply a stop for no reason. You have died. I can't make sense of it. I can't be at peace with it. It is profoundly unsettling and disturbing and there are no answers. Sometimes I just want to go berserk with the frustration of it all. WHY, WHY, WHY? There are no answers. There are no answers. There will never be any answers. I think constantly about your death, the manner of your death, the fact I don't know where you are or whether in fact you exist in any shape or form.

This state of mind could drive me mad if I let it. I feel I'm walking a tightrope of sanity. I am just about staying on the rope but I am wobbling all the time, about to fall off.

We are now in Cornwall, at Gillan Creek. I am lying in bed and the rain is dripping outside. We are in our safe place, together with the extended family, but you are not here and that is so hard. This time last year we were all together. Everything is the same and everything is different. The house is the same, the beach is the same, the cowrie shells are here and we're still fanatically looking for them, Grandpa is here watching the TV, the creek is still here, but you are not here so everything is different.

I'm going into a sort of numbness again about it all. We've brought your picture with us — the one in a lovely frame that we had at the wake — and we bring you offerings every day. A skeleton leaf, a feather, pretty stones, cowrie shells, little winkles, lichens, flowers. This morning I stood with a cup of tea looking at your picture and it just felt unreal. I still can't believe it. Kate is wonderful; it really helps having her around. She talks about it, she gets the intensity of it and embraces that. She told me that

Tess told her that she feels that, for her, this holiday will be the time that you really die. The annual summer holiday was always the time you cousins were together, year in, year out, for over twenty years. I just wish you were here — your gentle presence among us. We miss you so very, very much.

I am struggling with being on holiday because, of course, holidays are supposed to be a happy time, and come with that expectation. I walk up to the Herra, a small headland at the mouth of the creek where there is a tiny rocky beach with shingle, shells and a cave. I search for cowries, quietly absorbed. I find two, and feel cheered. Then I lie down, close my eyes, and listen to the sea as it swishes back and forth over the pebbles. I am enjoying the solitude and think-ing about Felix when some people come along and start skimming stones. I try to tune them out but without suc-cess, so I get up and continue along the coast path towards Nare Point. There is a beach I've kayaked to before and I wonder if there might be a way down to it. I keep my eyes peeled and, sure enough, I spot a little path through a hedge that twists down and then along the top of a rather alarming drop, before descending to a rocky beach with a reef and numerous inlets. I pick my way, trying to tread on the barnacles on the last bit of the rocky route, to avoid slipping. I make it down the rather perilous route safely and find a wide, empty beach that feels like a desert island. It has an abandoned feel, with lots of flotsam and jetsam, including an old lobster pot and many shells, in particular painted topshells, twinkling purple, green and silver.

By now I am rather hot and itching to get in the water. I strip off and get in without bothering with a swimsuit.

It's liberating to be naked. I immediately see a very chunky, handsome brown-and-black-striped wrasse swim past. I loll around in the water for a while, enjoying being totally alone. Then I get out and sit on the beach. I'm just texting Kate when I hear a snort. I look up and there is a large seal just offshore. I wonder if it has been playing grandmother's footsteps with me all along, while I was swimming in blissful ignorance. We look at each other. It almost feels as though it wanted to attract my attention. Is the seal actually Felix saying hello from wherever he is now?

The next day we decide to go to Nanjizal, a beach I have wanted to go for years, after first seeing a photo of it on a wild swimming website. There is a cave there with a tall, narrow arch, like the eye of a needle, with a turquoise pool in front of it. It's near Land's End, and Alex and I set off about 9 a.m. to get there at low tide, which is at about 10. As we drive, 'Angels' by Robbie Williams comes on the radio, setting me off into tears as I start thinking about funerals.

We get to the village from where we are going to walk to Nanjizal. The path goes through an ancient farm with a free library, where we stop and I get a book. We pass old granite buildings, go through a potato field and along the top of a heather- and gorse-covered valley, dazzling in yellow and purple. Then we get a glimpse of a stunning turquoise sea, and my heart lifts. The sea shimmers – the essence of turquoise. Then the arch, like a slit, becomes visible, and the azure pool in front of it is there: magical, like an enchanted place, something out of a fairy tale.

We get down to the beach and find it is strewn with enormous boulders. We clamber over them to the pool. The water is gin-clear, with white sand, really white sand; perhaps this is why the colour of the water is so extraordinary? I plunge in and put my head under to find the most vivid palette of purples, pinks and reds, stripy rocks, seaweed in an array of colours, and plump scarlet anemones. I feel as though I'm in a large natural baptismal font, cleansed – I don't know – purified almost.

Afterwards we seek out nearby Carn Brea, the biggest hill in the area, said to be the first and last hill in Britain. It's a place Alex has long wanted to go. There is a large beacon at the top – a metal basket on a pole, which is lit every year to mark the summer solstice. In the past it was tended by a succession of hermits, who kept a beacon burning for travellers and ships. The site is a place of late Neolithic and Bronze Age burials, with the remains of a large cairn at the top. We think about the remains of these ancient people, laid to rest here in this commanding spot. We can see all around, to Land's End and over to the Isles of Scilly.

We go back to the house and I have an early-evening kayak with Lucian up to the head of the creek. The sun is out and we paddle towards it in the lush, quiet greenness of the water, passing egrets, swans and gulls. We remember Felix being here last year. He spent most of the time in his room, but enjoyed looking for sea glass on the beach for Kate's collection. He was not at his happiest at that time. He was, I think, feeling anxious about the future, lacking in confidence about his plans. Little did we all know that actually his return to university was going to be a great success – he would go on stage, be part of a community.

That night before I go to sleep, I feel a total and utter sense of sadness and desperation. It is so strong it prevents me from sleeping and I just feel completely at a loss. Eventually, after about three hours, I get to sleep, but then wake up really early. It is quite frightening: a sense of being totally overwhelmed by misery.

I decide to go for a walk to Dennis Head, where I am hoping to find my brother Matthew, who is fishing off the headland. It is on the other side of the creek, and I ford the water, which is very easy because we are on spring tides and the creek is virtually dry. I stop and look in the old granite church of St Anthony-in-Meneage. I kneel down and say a prayer for Felix, then one for me and one for the rest of the family. Yes, I am an agnostic, but I am finding that Felix's death is forcing me to seek comfort in religion, despite myself. Then I look around and notice two carved wooden depictions of the Last Supper. Both are very old – fourteenth or fifteenth century. One is a three-dimensional carving; the other is a panel, the figures in relief, with Judas just a faint echo, peeping out from behind one of the apostles. It is made of dark-brown wood, black almost – ancient. There are carved angels on the fifteenth-century font, four of them – rough little people, not like angels at all, but like four Celts.

I leave some money in the donations box and then set off uphill towards the end of the headland, looking at the empty creek below, a trickle of water disappearing into the trees. I find a fisherman's path, down which I suspect Matthew might be, but I decide against following it as it is steep and narrow, and bordered by thorny bushes. I would get badly scratched and he might not be there anyway. I turn back and head towards Helford, past fat sloes in the bushes on the right and an electric fence on the left. Great expanses of the estuary become visible, and I am struck by how it looks like a much bigger version of Gillan Creek, an *Alice in Wonderland* version of it. I remember kayaking there with Felix in previous years. There was one time when the winds were very strong, coming from the west, which meant we had a real struggle as we paddled in from the open sea.

It starts to rain as I enter a wood and walk downhill, glimpses of the green water below. I reach Ponsence Cove, where the sand is brown and wet – increasingly wet. Someone has created an enormous cairn out of flat slates, as high as me. It's now raining hard and I shelter under a rocky outcrop in the cliff. The rain shows no sign of stopping so I just walk along the beach in the rain. I look for cowries but don't find any, although I do find some very pretty pink conical topshells the colour of strawberries and cream. It then really starts to chuck it down, and I manage to find a hollow in the cliff – it would be pushing it to call it a cave – where I crouch, looking out at the bleak and blustery beach. Despite the rain, the sea is clear and inviting, and green under the overhanging trees of the twisted wood that borders it. The water draws me and I want to swim, but I don't, as the thought of getting changed in the deluge is too much. I visit the cairn before leaving, to add a stone for Felix, and discover that it's not actually a cairn, but hollow, like an igloo.

3 August

The holiday feels like an emotional rollercoaster. The trouble is, most places I go have memories of you. This is tricky, but it is also a good thing, because I need those memories. Your photo is now surrounded with myriad offerings: cowries, winkles, cockle shells, seaweed, stones. I found a very smooth black stone shaped like a kidney, which I put there. Today I found a heart-shaped piece of glass on the beach. I shall add it.

I thought it might be a nice idea to talk about you over dinner. I lit the candles by your photograph and then announced my idea to everyone (a mistake to announce it, in retrospect), saying it would be nice if people wanted to share their memories. I started by talking about remembering you lying on the sand at Kynance Cove reading your book. Then Kate mentioned you getting your 'midnight milk' and then that was it – conversation fizzled out and everyone felt awkward. Chat gradually resumed and the subject was not mentioned again.

After dinner, I cried. The idea of talking about you was a failure. I just don't want to feel you are forgotten. You are part of our family and I want that to be acknowledged. It feels so strange to be sitting having dinner on holiday, laughing and chatting together, and not mentioning the elephant in the room – the fact that we're all missing you dreadfully and feel so traumatised, so empty inside.

I'm thinking about the months passing since you died. It's now five months. I don't want the months to pass. I want it all to be very recent. Then I'd be closer to the time you were still here, alive, getting involved in university life, growing, gaining new experiences, living. I don't want time to move on because I feel under pressure to get back to normal, to feel less grief – but why should I? I want to return to the time when you were still alive.

We are going to set off a flotilla of boats in memory of Felix. It's all come about by accident, really. Matthew and Kate had a minor clash and it resulted in them having a conversation about everyone feeling sad because Felix is not here. Kate and I were talking and she said she felt we should 'do' something. She suggested making boats and setting them alight. I immediately thought, *Great idea*. A much better idea, in fact, than talking about Felix over dinner.

Kate makes a beautiful boat out of twigs, with a letter to Felix that acts as the sail. I try to make a Moses basket out of twigs and dried leaves. I want to launch it with a sea-urchin skeleton inside to represent Felix as a baby – a sweet swaddled oval – but my efforts fail and I have to abandon that plan. Instead, I make a raft with two sails, which I'm actually quite pleased with in the end, and a paper boat into which I put two cowries and some flowers. Alex also makes a paper boat decorated with flowers, and Lucian makes a wonderfully sturdy vessel out of wood. My three nieces really get into it, being the creative creatures they are. Cosy's boat starts life as an egg box, but you wouldn't know it; it is transformed into the most graceful galleon, with a message on the sail. Ruby makes an elegant origami lotus flower. Tess's boat is spectacular: a galleon made out of willow. My brother James's boats are large and bold, made out of beer boxes. He describes one as a 'ship of the line' and the other a 'long ship'.

We assemble them all on a big table outside the house and admire them. Then we process to the beach, where dusk is falling. We put nightlights in each boat and set them off one by one. Magically, they all float, and they drift away, the little lights moving into the distance. Then James appears with his two boats ablaze, and launches them, great boxes of flames, dramatic and ceremonial. We stand there in the growing darkness, watching the barely-moving water, like black oil in the twilight, on which float the boats. We stare as they move further and further away, and the lights gradually go out.

Being there

31 August

Today is the twentieth anniversary of Princess Diana's death and of course it is leading the bulletins. Everyone's remembering where they were when they heard the news. Of course, twenty years ago you were six months old; that was such a special year, 1997. The year of your birth, us becoming parents, having this beautiful baby in our life, our lives changed for ever. A time of such busyness, such hope, such disruption, such change; we'd created a new life — it was unimaginably beautiful and amazing as well as being rather terrifying and extremely exhausting and, actually, full of worry, because your early weeks were so difficult. And now it's all over.

The weather is turning. The rain has been incessant. The

Dart is in spate, like an overstretched muscle, powering along in intense, angry twists. Yesterday my friend Rachel and I, along with Yaara, went to Ladies Pool but swimming was impossible as the river raged by like a train, sweeping along everything in its path. However, there was a foaming eddy by Black Rock, where we got in and swirled around in the water, which was like black tea. We were surrounded by large bubbles on the surface, like empty snow domes, which kept expanding and bursting.

Over in Torbay, where I've been working, there have been dramatic steel skies and strong winds. My immediate reaction is displeasure, but then I think, No, embrace it, perhaps it is more appropriate to my mood: angry, dark sea. That is rather fitting; perhaps that is just as therapeutic as calm, sunny, blue conditions. Embrace the distress: will this be the right way to approach autumn and winter, never my favourite seasons?

We've decided to get a dog. It's something I've been obsessing over since Felix died, looking endlessly at rescue dogs on websites and researching the different breeds. I desperately need comfort, I really do; I want something to love, to distract me, to get me out of bed every day. I also think we need something to unite around as a family; we need some glue to stick us back together. At the moment we are three people stuck in our individual grooves of grief, not communicating that much.

We have an appointment to see a labradoodle puppy at a farm near Okehampton, on the northern side of Dartmoor. Alex, Lucian and I decide to go for a walk first; it's a walk I love that goes from the dull roar of the A30 and its dreary road bridges past a huge man-made lake and then up alongside a bubbling rocky river and up to one of

Dartmoor's highest tors. We park at Meldon Reservoir and head past the lake, with its romantic-looking island, a picture of pastoral peace. And yet its creation, in 1972, was ugly. The Dartmoor Preservation Association described the flooding of the valley as 'the murder of a friend' and Stanley Johnson wrote a piece in the *Spectator* headlined 'The Rape of Dartmoor'. Now, the lake and huge dam seem like part of the scenery, with this violent history largely forgotten. Eric Hemery, in his book *High Dartmoor: Land and People*, describes it as 'a place of stern, almost classical beauty . . . we have lost Meldon Gorge . . . yet in its stead have gained something no less remarkable.'

The lake is beautiful, but as I walk past, I feel sad at the destruction of the river that once was here. We reach Vellake Corner, which is the point at which the river was altered to make the reservoir. Here the passage of the West Okement river is rudely blocked by a weir. There is a flat area along one side where ponies graze. We go over to a marshy place where sundews grow – Dartmoor's answer to the Venus flytrap. We squat down to examine them. They are fascinating: tiny, green-centred plants with red tentacles, each with a blob on the end that looks like a drop of water or dew. These little droplets attract insects, which then get stuck on the plant before being slowly digested by the plant's enzymes.

We start to ascend alongside the West Okement, its gurgling and bubbling a constant hum in the background, larks singing above our heads. This part of the river is known as Valley of Rocks, with the water tumbling headlong down through a procession of boulders; a vibrant, lush, living place. We reach a pair of oak trees on the left, our secret signpost to a pool below that we discovered on a previous visit. We scramble down through the bracken and dead oak leaves that carpet the ground, and change into our swim stuff, eager to get into the small pool that is surrounded by enormous, moss-covered rocks.

The boulders really are huge. We sit in the pool and they tower above us, with the water crashing down through a gap between them. We brace against the flow and sub-merge, our faces kissed by the bubbles. There's even a 'room' – a cavity in between some of the rocks, with 'win-dows', where we sit being pummelled by the water.

After our swim, we keep climbing until we reach Black-a-Tor Copse, one of Dartmoor's three ancient dwarf woods, with its twisted, stunted oaks and luxuriant ferns and mosses. For a while, we wander, losing ourselves in this little green world. We are together but apart, a family changed, not talking about the absence of Felix, but feeling it all the time. His death is just too much to talk about; there is a sense that if we do, that then perhaps everything could descend into total chaos. But being together, wandering around this magical little wood, is a comfort. After, we climb still higher, to Black Tor, from where we can see for miles: across to North Devon and down to Bodmin Moor.

Back in the car, we set the satnav to the breeders and soon roll up at a scruffy-looking farm with a sign saying 'Free Range Dogs. Do not come in. Sound your horn and wait.' We honk our horn and wait. Nothing happens. We honk again. Nothing happens. We ring the farm number and hear the bell of the phone echoing around the farm. Eventually someone appears, surrounded by dogs – all kinds of dogs, yapping and barking and running around.

We are led into a room in a barn and are introduced to Marmite, the mum, and two of her puppies, from which we are to choose. They are both female, little black blobs of furry deliciousness. They are both so tiny and sweet. We choose the one with the tighter curls. I cradle her in my lap, feeling her warmth and vulnerability. I can't wait to bring her home, but that won't be for a few weeks.

The next day I spend doing domestic tasks: tidying up, cooking. I make an apple and blackberry pie, and a lemon tart, and I think about the difference between grief and depression. I have had some severe spells of depression in the past, and I know that if I were depressed, I wouldn't be able to make a pie. But grief – well, I can. It's more a state of existence than an illness. It is a changed state of existence in which you feel desperately sad and frequently cry. Well, at least I do. Of course, there are different levels of intensity to the grief, and at the beginning, when Felix died, my functioning was badly affected. But, strangely, now, I don't think I'm depressed, just in a profound state of grief.

And yet . . . I am not writing Felix as many letters as I have been. Mainly, I suppose, because of working, which means I have less time, and less mental and emotional energy. I am struggling to keep pace with life 'normalising'. I am having to put my physical and emotional energies into working and surviving. The fact that I am writing fewer letters to Felix upsets me.

I receive a text from Ruby, my niece and Felix's cousin. She has been shortlisted for the Budleigh Salterton Literary Festival Creative Writing Prize, with a poem she wrote about being at Felix's funeral and thinking back to happier times. She'd shown me the poem a while back; I found it deeply moving and was struck by its imagery. She's been shortlisted in the adult category even though

she's only seventeen. She's been invited to the award ceremony, so she's coming down to stay.

We head off to Budleigh Salterton which is on the East
Devon coast, a very well-heeled and picturesque town
with a long pebble beach. We find the hall where the
ceremony is happening and head in, wondering what the
evening holds. They announce the results in reverse order,
and when the judge says '. . . and the winner is only seventeen' we know she's won and are overwhelmed. We cry,
full of both joy and terrible sadness that Felix's death has
led to this. We feel embarrassed about the crying, because
people don't know the backstory. There is nothing in the
poem actually spelling out that it is about Felix's death.
Nobody around us in this crowded room knows about the
trauma that has led to this moment.

Afterwards, we wander along the pebble shore, not
really sure what to do or what to feel.

The following morning, I drive Ruby to Exeter to get
the train home. I see a young man of about Felix's age and
height walking along the street and feel a lurch of pain. I
manage not to cry in the car. Later, back home, I keep on
crying in great uncontrollable bursts, like a tidal wave of
grief hitting me all over again.

Being There
(One Summer's Day)

There's a sudden shift in the air.
The first note prises open a crack in time and all in a
moment I'm standing in the heat of one summer's day.
A searing warmth nearly as deep as the
red in my cheeks.

Being there

There's an August feeling.
Stepping onto the balcony, eyes skim and stop on
the horizon, sinking slate.
Buddleia, heavy with a scent so sickly sweet the
layers of butterflies become tacky like our fingers,
doused in a
honey glaze.
In the shallows of the sea we dive for oddities
uncovered with such an instantaneous glee shown
in the arcs of
our mouths as we swim back home.
To escape the chill we fumble with the showers
until the hot pellets graze in burning streaks.
There's a sudden shift in the summer.
The boundaries have fallen on the shoreline.
Waist deep we wade, rigid as the sea frigid
But he stops and sits on the sand.
This is how it would normally be but something
is different.
We retreat, pack up, drive off, move forwards
But he just sits and looks, then picks up his daily book.
And then I'm back again.
Standing on top of the hill where the wind cuts
sharp, like the stark black keys on white
Their contrast a jarring battle waging war with
our emotions.
But his brother tames them softly.
He unwrinkles them in a tune so smooth it pierces
you in an unwarranted mix of beauty and sadness.
I think about where he is now,
Both below in the earth and skywards above
An encapsulation, safe with the strength of his hug.

I've felt this before.
In the cool of the summer night we slipped
ourselves into the water.
The world ushered into a drawling darkness,
disturbed only by gentle baptism.
Our fingers set the sea alight in tiny fragments like
sprightly iron filings.
We carved our way through liquid starlight
a rippling mirror
And as the elements lost all definition the lucidity
intensified with a scintillation all around us.
The merging of the sea and sky and he's with us again,
in the brilliance of one summer's night.

20 September

Last night I went with Yaara to see Beautiful, *a musical about the life of Carole King, who of course you won't have heard of but she's a celebrated singer-songwriter responsible for one of the best-selling albums ever, called* Tapestry. *Amanda and I listened to her incessantly, along with k.d. lang and Tracy Chapman, when we lived together in the nineties.*

Anyway, there's a particular song of hers, 'So Far Away', that I cannot get out of my head since last night. When the song was sung on stage in the theatre, I felt such a strong ache in my heart and I cannot erase the lyrics from my head. It breaks my heart — I'm welling up as I write this. You are so far away; in fact, you are not anywhere at all. And that line about seeing your face at the door. How I wish I could see your beautiful face again. But I never will.

I do think a lot about suicide. How it is something I would quite like to do. But I can't do it. I just couldn't do that to Lucian and Alex, and make everything worse, much as I'd like to. It's just so hard to keep going through the intolerable pain. Last night, as I slid into bed beside Alex after getting home late from the theatre, I started heaving and crying and my body went all tense, and I just felt so desperate, like an animal in pain, trembling – awful. Sometimes I honestly wonder how I can carry on. I'm drinking too much but I don't really care. Nothing much matters apart from keeping things steady for Lucian. I'm dreading my birthday. I think it's increasing the emotional turbulence. I don't want to celebrate another year of life. Friends are asking what I want to do and I don't really know or care.

In the end my birthday goes quite well. Right up until the day before, I don't know what I want to do. Usually, I have a swim with friends around Burgh Island, a tiny half-tidal island just off the South Devon coast, but I just don't know if I'm in the mood for that. It seems wrong that Felix won't be there. But then I suddenly decide I *do* want to do it. The decision is largely dictated by the fact that if I don't organise anything, I will be on my own all day as Alex and Lucian are away looking at Durham University.

Esther, Ellie, Rachel, Milla, Catherine, Caroline, Theresa and I meet first thing at Bigbury-on-Sea as it is high water at 08:30. It is beautifully wild, with swiftly passing grey clouds against a blue sky. The sun is coming up and gleaming on the sea, which does, however, look rather swelly and lumpy. Undeterred, we walk onto the beach, entering the water where the waves crash against each other at the front of the island. We wade, feeling the soft ridges of sand between our toes. As the water gets higher up our bodies, we smile and laugh, happy in the anticipation of this annual ritual. I feel so grateful for my friends, and the familiarity and comfort of my birthday tradition. When the water is chest height, we start to swim, heading for the left-hand side of the island. It is a spring tide, so there is a lot of water about, and it fills the gap between the islet of Murray's Rock, with its little iron post, and the island itself. We swim through the channel, above the swirling kelp, and then turn right and through a gully to the Mermaid Pool. This is a pool for the guests of the island hotel, created out of a natural lagoon in the rocks and finished off with concrete walls filling in the gaps. The hotel has new owners, who have put barbed wire over the top of the walls, but we slide under the wire and swim around in the oasis of calm, being watched from the hotel by people with binoculars. I feel held and supported by my friends and the water.

Not wishing to outstay our welcome, we climb out and swim back along the gully before anyone can come and tell us off. Some decide to swim back to the beach, while Ellie, Catherine, Esther, Theresa and I carry on. The sea is active and full of swell but we persist, hoping that we might be able to get around the back of the island. There is a spectacular channel, dubbed Death Valley years ago by Amanda, which we normally swim through. It is stunning, with great slate sides and a seabed full of rocks, colourful seaweed and fish, often with a chorus line of cormorants standing watching. However, today there is a fearsome eddy just in front of it that is sending waves in all directions, threatening to sweep us onto the rocks, so we decide to be sensible and head back like the others.

Later, at home, my mood descends again. Swimming

with my beloved friends was a temporary high, a wonderful interlude. But I still can't prevent the frightening thoughts about taking my own life. I just think it would be easier if I weren't here. There would be no more pain. I would no longer have to deal with this loss every day, day in, day out.

I find myself thinking quite calmly and rationally about how I would do it. Pills would be the obvious thing. Or I could drown myself with rocks in the Dart, which could be quite effective. It is a strange sort of comfort to entertain these thoughts – the idea that there is an escape if I really want it. Knowing there is a way out is a perverse relief. But at the same time, I know I just could not do that to my family and friends.

25 September

My precious Felix, as I was leaving work today, I just couldn't stop thinking about the fact I will never be able to hug you again. I'll never be able to hold you, to stroke your cheek or your hair; I'll never again experience that physicality of you. It just breaks my heart; I just cannot comprehend it, I cannot accept it. As I drove home, I wept and wept, and in the privacy of the car allowed my face to contort into shapes of utter misery. I realise that the majority of the time I am trying not to feel miserable and devastated. Resisting it all the time is hard work.

I've decided I'm going to drop a day. Working full-time just doesn't give me enough time with you. It doesn't leave me with any down time, empty time, to grieve. I think a lot of the grieving is an inactive process, but it does need space and time to happen. Writing is a form of active grieving, I think, but since I've been working, I've not been writing so much, and it's because I don't have the mental and temporal space for it to happen. I'm simply too tired after a day's work. I cannot allow you to fade because I am devoting too much time to work. Writing to you and thinking about you is the only way I can maintain my relationship with you and I'm damned if I'm going to let work get in the way of that.

I think about you such a lot. And yet my grip on you IS loosening. I can't bear for you to slip away — I must resist that. There's a ghastly conflict between your vitality, the reality of your presence in my life, and the growing realisation that you are extinct, over, part of the past, lying dead in the ground.

The mountain

4 October

My dearest darling, yesterday I went to the dentist. It turned out part of a tooth had broken off and I'd lost some of the filling. The dentist decided to fix it there and then. I was fine, sitting in the chair and chatting. Then the needle went in and it HURT as usual, but suddenly, I found myself weeping violently. I was unhinged; it was awful. I was sitting in the dentist's chair howling, which was quite embarrassing as obviously, on the face of it, it was a complete overreaction. But it was as though the physical pain had punched a hole in the armour shielding the emotional pain of your death and it all flooded out in one fell swoop. The people in the dentist were lovely but I just felt so destabilised. I carried on and had the filling but the

minute I got home, once I was through the front door, I col-
lapsed crying again.

It's been building up, I think. We're clearing the house and
making it ready for the arrival of the puppy. It's exhausting,
physically and emotionally. Our fundraising climb of Ben Nevis
is looming, which I am excited about, but it is also an emotion-
ally challenging thing to do, celebrating you and remembering you
publicly, and I am worried about how I am going to feel on the
big day.

Tonight, I went to Ladies Pool with Yaara, which helped. As
we walked along the river, I noticed the leaves had started to turn.
There were dots of bright yellow on the ground and waves of
bright green, orange and gold overhead. The river had calmed
down a bit. It is still a rushing torrent and very high, but Ladies
Pool was swimmable. Yaara forgot her costume so we went in
starkers and swam around talking in the fading light. There was
no sun on the pool but we could see it as it was dropping rapidly
behind the trees further upstream. That smooth, silky, dark water
was just what I needed and I felt better when I got out.

I'm thinking a lot about duality at the moment: my double
life. On the face of it I am functioning, going to work,
smiling at things, generally being normal, but underneath
I am wracked with emptiness and pain. I'm like a spy, with
a hidden life. Along with that is the fact that Felix's death
is something I need to talk about, explore, express, but I
don't want to bore or burden my friends. Maybe I should
find a support group? I don't want counselling – I don't
think I have a psychological problem I need to solve – and
I don't want to talk to someone who, however well qualified and well meaning, has no idea what it's like to lose a

child. I know now that if this hadn't happened to me, I would simply have had no idea what it's like. I know there are support groups for parents who have lost children, but the thought of turning up at some church hall or somewhere, and talking to people I don't know, fills me with absolute dread. And, selfishly, I don't want to hear about other people's pain. Maybe I'll just have to plod on alone.

The weekend of the big climb is here. Most of our gang fly to Inverness, where we are met by our friend Simon, who's already here. We're a close-knit group and have been climbing the country's various peaks together over the last few years. First, we did Snowdon, then we did Scafell Pike, and the third plan was always to do Ben Nevis. Then Felix died, and now the Ben Nevis plan has become a memorial fundraiser for him and for the charity SUDEP Action.

It is late afternoon and we head off from the airport and drive alongside Loch Ness, where we pull in to a layby and pile out of the cars to have a swim. The water is dark and smooth, with rowan trees on the bank, their berries crimson against the black water. We are surrounded by mountains.

The next day, we are blessed with lovely weather for our climb. The sun is out and it is dry. The path is like a super-highway of walkers, including one chap doing it in high heels, 'for a challenge'. It is extraordinarily hard work. I am red as a beetroot as we get higher and higher.

About a third of the way up is Lochan Meall an t-Suidhe, also known (inaccurately) as the Halfway Lochan. Simon, Judy and I stop here while the others continue the ascent. The lake is long, a flat, shiny oval set among featureless moorland. Standing at the edge is like gazing into an infinity pool, with the tips of mountains just visible across the distant surface. I stand there, taking a deep breath, feeling exhausted but also excited, and strangely calmed by this otherworldly place.

We're swimming here for Felix. For Judy, in particular, it is a supreme sacrifice as she hates cold water and normally only swims in the Mediterranean. This is her first swim in UK waters for twenty-five years. But she is determined to do it, to raise money for SUDEP Action. Wrongly, I assume it will be quite warm (for me, at least), as the loch is pretty shallow. But it's actually perishingly cold – I would guess about 8 degrees or less. The reason, I suppose, is the altitude: we're 570 metres above sea level. We all grit our teeth and take the plunge, with Judy, in particular, producing a spectacular range of yelps and grimaces. I thought I'd be swimming the full half-mile length of the lake but there's no way that's happening; it's way too cold. But here we are, halfway up a Scottish mountain, in a remote body of water away from everything, the icy cut of the loch water on our bodies, embracing that pain of Felix's death – feeling it, feeling our loss. I thank God for my friends.

The following day we have a dramatic walk through a mountain pass with glowering, changeable weather, on the old military road along the West Highland Way. As we walk, I feel my mood sink. There is nothing I can do; I can just feel it happening. It draws me down like a lead weight. I start to cry, manage to hide it, and then to stop. Later, coming back down a slippery path, I fall over and get very upset, dissolving into tears. It's a bit like the time in the dentist – I'm heaving-crying all over again, excessive tears triggered by a small accident.

On the way back, we stop by a promontory on Loch Leven overlooking a trio of islets including Eilean Munde, where Saint Fintan came from Iona in the seventh century and built a chapel. Much later the isle was used as a burial place for three different clans. I love the idea of it being a holy island, where the dead are remembered. We decide to swim. The water in the loch is wonderfully black, but very clear at the edge. We swim over huge, shiny ribbons of kelp, with lots of tiny fishes darting about. Then I spot a great pink orb, glowing like a lamp underwater. It's an urchin, and there is a tiny baby starfish attached to the weed next to it.

12 October

Guess what, darling, we now have a puppy – Tarka. She is the most adorable black ball of fluff. She arrived on Monday (it is now Thursday) and we had two nights of whining and howling but amazingly she settled last night and made no sound at all. You would love her. She is a labradoodle – ¾ miniature poodle and ¼ Labrador, and is just the cutest thing. It is sudden, intense love and my feelings are quite mixed: joy, of course, at having a furry baby to love, and be loved by, but sadness that you're not here to meet her, and that your death is partly the reason we got her. She is certainly a distraction, which was another reason for getting her. I haven't had much time to think about you in the last few days, which is good and bad – good that I have been distracted from my grief, bad in that I need to think about you and to grieve. Hopefully it will all balance out. She is helping. Somehow, my mood is better. It's hard to describe: there's a sort of contentment that's there. It's made me realise how much every day has been a struggle to carry on, it really has. Somehow the puppy takes the edge off that, gives life a lightness. I feel a lot less anxious. She is a ball of fun and energy which lifts the mood.

A few days ago I called in at the abbey and lit candles for you and Grandma. I was overwhelmed again by the shocking injustice of your death – your life snuffed out just as things were starting to get better for you. Before I entered the church, I started reliving the day we brought you there the night before your funeral. Walking towards the abbey and seeing the hearse, and feeling sick and frightened. The boys carrying you through the silence of the empty church, up past the pews and the Lady Chapel, where I light candles for you now, and through to the Blessed Sacrament Chapel, where Kate and Grandpa were waiting in the dim candlelight. Father Francis saying prayers, and our small group, dwarfed by the hugeness of the chapel, sobbing and snuffling and not really taking anything in. And having to leave you there, alone, the night before your funeral and burial.

Autumn is now in full swing and I have a heavy cold and a chesty cough, and am generally feeling depleted. This is the first time I have been ill since Felix died seven months ago, which seems quite remarkable. I have been thinking a lot about the tension between life continuing, moving on, and my desire for everything to stop, to stay still in the moment of Felix's loss. It's a tension between joy and sorrow, between the fact that there are still wonderful things about life, and the ever-present hell of losing my child. They seem incompatible, but they aren't really. Life has always been full of ups and downs and contradictions; it's just that now they are grossly magnified, intensified.

Last night, while trying to get to sleep, I kept thinking

about Felix lying in the chapel of rest at the funeral parlour, his hair strangely set in place, his face childlike. I
suddenly realised I was visualising his face as pale as alabas-
ter, when, in fact, it was dark, almost black, and mottled
in death. This made me weep, the thought of his strange,
darkened face. It also made me think of my mother in her
final hours, as she lay there on her deathbed, motionless,
yellowing, a shadow of her former self. I thought of all the
pain she went through, that terrible drawn-out death from
cancer, in contrast to Felix's. I realise now that, at the
time, I simply had no concept of the pain she must have
been enduring, I think because I had not experienced
it myself. Now that I have, and although the pain is
different – it is emotional, not physical – I can imagine the
intensity is similar.

A photo on my desk shows my mother reading Felix a
story. He sits on her lap, with his golden helmet of hair,
looking intensely at the pages. They are both gone. I weep
again.

An All Souls' ritual is held every November at the Green
Hill. I decide to attend, and Maria and Yaara come with
me. It is the most awe-inspiring moonlit night. A huge,
white moon hangs like a lamp in the sky, illuminating the
lines of graves and the full river below. Mist hangs over the
valley. Owls keep on hooting. The burial ground is dotted
with night lights, one on every grave. At Felix's grave, we
add more candles so we can see his name in the slate headstone. We stand there and look down towards the river.
People are gathering around a blazing fire, and then the
ceremony starts. It is very simple, and led by the undertakers who manage the site, Ru and Claire. Ru speaks. He is

a poet. He speaks about continuity, the earth, the ancestors, winter, sleep, memory. What he is saying has true resonance, which churns up my emotions, and I find it hard to stay quiet, to stem my tears, not to make a noise. Claire also says a few words, then they read out the names of all the people buried there, including, of course, Felix. Then we are all invited to throw a pinecone on the fire and to say something if we wish. Lots of people do, including a woman who says the pinecone is for the seven children she miscarried who weren't honoured or remembered back then, when her babies died. Then Ru announces that someone will sing and I think, *Oh God, we're going to have 'Kumbaya'*, but actually the singer has the most beautiful voice. She starts without words and then everyone ends up singing a very simple refrain about remembering. I don't sing, though. I know if I do, I will completely break down.

All this week the moon has been shining so brightly. The day before yesterday I took Tarka up to Cold East Cross on the moor. We got there at quarter to six in the evening, and already the moon was up and sending a sharp gleam over the gorse and heather, while there were still wisps of sunset over to the west. We walked in the gloaming and I had some moments of peace, held in a sort of limbo place, full of grey shadows.

The first Christmas

12 November

I feel I am back in a more specific state of mourning again. I'm feeling very internalised – I don't really want to go out into the world, I want to hide at home. I want to think about you. I don't wish to preoccupy myself with external issues.

I am still quite ill. My asthma has become really bad as a result of the cold, which went to my chest. My breathing is shallow and tight, and I'm coughing a lot. I feel absolutely drained.

Maria's mum died. She was very old and it was not unexpected. I went to the funeral at Ashprington church and the burial afterwards at the Green Hill, which in retrospect I think was a mistake. It was only a small group and I wanted to be there for Maria, but it was hard. As soon as I set foot in the ancient church, I started crying, and I cried pretty much through the whole service. When we got to the Green Hill it was exceptionally beautiful, with the sun shining. I calmed down a bit but was still pretty distraught.

I think lots of things are conspiring at the moment, the most obvious of which is Christmas. It is looming dreadfully. I am absolutely dreading it. I've been worrying about it; I can't bear the thought of you not being there, of not buying you a present. Oh I just can't bear it. We have discussed it. It's just going to be us. We will go to Mass and then we will visit you at the Green Hill. That's given me an idea. I'm going to get you a little Christmas tree. That's cheered me up, actually.

The autumn leaves are so beautiful this year. I've had a couple of walks and swims along the Dart surrounded by swathes of oranges, golds, yellows, bronzes and coppers, with banks of leaves piling up. They remind me of my childhood in the Chilterns. We would walk to a place I used to call the Light Garden; I've no idea why I called it that. I remember the exposed chalk of the hills along the path. The chalk was covered by huge piles of beech leaves, which Grandpa would roll us in. It is such a strong, happy memory — it really stands out in the mind map of my childhood: a sunlit glade of white and gold. I hope you had that kind of childhood. I wonder if you have any concept of it now. Does any of it matter any more?

It's 9 p.m. on a Tuesday night and I am about to get in the shower, when I am suddenly gripped by a terrible, utter terror at Felix's death. It's a sudden, breathless dread at the hideous enormity of his young death. It is just incomprehensible. I feel desperate, desperate, desperate. It's unutterably dreadful. I feel just a bit insane.

The clocks went back a few weeks ago and the darkness

has been increasing noticeably, and with it a corresponding darkness inside me. I am regularly gripped by inner dread and horror; it's a sort of cold chill that goes through me with no warning. It can happen any time – I might be walking down the stairs or sitting at my desk. It doesn't seem to happen outside, only at home. Outside, I suppose there are distractions. I am out in the world – the world and its busyness takes over; or, if I am out on the moor or beside the sea, their vastness takes over – it is bigger than anything I can feel. But inside, I am in the family space where there is a gaping hole, a yawning abyss of emptiness.

Work has been intense this week and I am shredded by the time I finish on Thursday. I have too much to drink and then check my email in bed to find a picture Kate has sent me that I've never seen before. It is of Felix and me on a beach in Cornwall, both reading. I am sitting up and Felix is lying down, resting his head on my lap. You can see how close we are. I cry myself to sleep.

The following day all I want to do is stay in bed, but it's too cold. I make a fire and sit in front of the telly all day. I just let time pass. I feel so wobbly. It is the same on Saturday, except friends are coming for supper so towards the end of the afternoon I have to get my act together for that. It helps, actually, and we have a lovely evening.

On Sunday I am less wobbly. My friend Ron is organising a campfire and moonlight 'Supermoon Swim' at Coryton Cove, so I decide to go. I want earth, air, fire, water; I want to feel small, lessened, dominated by something bigger than myself. As I drive over, there is a fiery sunset behind me that burns in the rear-view mirror. Then, as I approach the coast, the sky is filled with pink, smoky blotches and the ghost of an afternoon rainbow.

I arrive at the beach and there is quite a crowd but no one I know really well, which is good, as I don't really want to talk to anyone. There are two fires going. To the right, a stand of trees is silhouetted on the headland. We swim in the last of the light, the sea grey and soft, and as I warm up by the fire, the night comes down. There are great blankets of cloud on the horizon, where the moon should be. Gradually, though, the supermoon bursts through in all its ice-white brilliance, smudging the clouds and then appearing in full, casting a ray of light onto the water. I come home feeling a degree of peace.

8 December

Last night as I was trying to get to sleep, images of you lying dead in your student room came to me unbidden – the horror of standing outside with the ambulance there and people looking awkward, not looking me in the face. Just horrific. Thank God I'm not haunted by this the entire time, but when it comes, my God it's awful.

I miss you all the time, every day. There's a huge hole at home but we limp on without you, not exactly holed below the water line, but sometimes it feels like that.

I have bought a little Christmas tree in a pot for you. We will put it by your grave next weekend. Kate and the girls have made some decorations out of dried oranges and kiwi fruits; they are beautiful, with little notes on them – beautiful, but oh so sad.

Anna, Yaara and I head to the Yealm Estuary for a swim. We park by the Ship pub at Noss Mayo. It is a low spring tide and we walk along the creek bed, squelching through the silt, looking up at the tide mark above us on the rocky shore. I see a flash of electric blue: a kingfisher. It disappears into a hole in the bank. I feel it is somehow an embodiment of Felix. As we walk along, we keep seeing great clumps of oyster shells. Soon we reach Kilpatrick Steps, where the estuary is swimmable. The water is grey and flat, with the boats all facing towards the sea. The tide is coming in and the current is very strong; so strong, in fact, that we wade through it then stop and let ourselves be pulled back upriver: a wonderful, restful feeling, being carried along by the primitive, moon-driven force of the water.

The following day, there is hazy sun, and Alex and I head out for a walk in the afternoon. The weather is dramatic and changeable. The sun is dropping all the time, sometimes masked by enormous swathes of clouds marching through, and sometimes shining brightly. The wind is exceptionally strong; it's been wuthering around the house for the last few hours. We climb up towards Sharp Tor, towards a small hawthorn tree silhouetted between the highest two lumps of rock. We get to the top and look over to the west where a great sunburst is coming down from above, rays splaying onto the magnificent Dart Gorge below. The view from here is spectacular, particularly of the Dart, buried in a richly wooded, deep cleft. From the top of Sharp Tor, we walk downhill towards Yar Tor and I notice a small rocky outcrop.

'Does that have a name?' I ask Alex.

'Yes,' he replies. 'Tiny Tor. Do you not remember Felix called it that?'

He told me we'd been on a walk when Felix was about nine and Lucian was about six, and we'd had exactly the same conversation, except that Felix had named the outcrop Tiny Tor. I have no recollection of this. We carry on towards Yar Tor, passing a well-preserved hut circle that isn't on the map. It reminds me of last Christmas Day, which was to be Felix's last Christmas, though we didn't know that at the time. Before Christmas dinner, we went for a walk on Buckland Common to look for a group of hut circles that had recently been rediscovered and were in the process of being cleared of bracken and scrub so they could be seen again. Back in the Bronze Age, this was quite a settlement, with several round houses that would have had stone bases with thatched roofs. All that remain now are the rings of stones; there are five or six of them in this settlement. We wandered around the site in the murky weather, and the boys excitedly ran off to find all the hut circles.

Later, back home, I am sitting in the kitchen threading cotton through dried orange slices that will decorate Felix's Christmas tree. 'Walk Out to Winter' by Aztec Camera comes on the radio – a happy, melodic tune, sung by a young male voice. It prompts a stab of pain at the loss of Felix, a beautiful young man. It also sends me tumbling back to my own youth. It seems to be the happy, optimistic songs that upset me most, not the sad ones. It's the contrast of the lightness and joy with what I'm feeling inside.

15 December

Christmas cards have started to arrive this week. They all say 'Dear Sophie, Alex and Lucian' – with no mention of you at all. The day the first one arrived, I was really shaken. It really upset me.

I'm trying to analyse why the lack of your name is upsetting me so much. It's such a graphic demonstration of your death. The day the first one arrived, I wanted to go on Facebook and say something like 'IF YOU WANT TO SEND ME A CHRISTMAS CARD, THAT IS LOVELY BUT PLEASE MENTION FELIX'S NAME AND ACKNOWLEDGE HIS EXISTENCE.' Would it be so hard for people to write something along the lines of 'You must be missing Felix so much'? I guess people are just too scared of writing the wrong thing. But writing nothing is worse. Yes, you are dead, but having your name left off Christmas cards feels like such a kick in the teeth. Perhaps I'm being oversensitive. After all, you are dead, you are no longer here, so why should people address you in a Christmas card?

Just because you're not here any more, doesn't mean you are not an integral part of our lives. This is the point. You may have died but you are still here in our family – in our minds, our hearts, our souls, our essence. You are part of us and always will be. I want to hear your name, see your name written down; I want your picture everywhere. You cannot be written out of existence.

It is Christmas Eve and I am missing Felix so terribly, terribly much. At 3 p.m. I listen to the carols from King's. This is an annual ritual that goes back to my childhood. It was an essential part of Christmas: we would listen to the carols while pottering in the kitchen, preparing the sprouts and so on. The familiarity and usual comfort of the ritual is still there but with a gaping difference: Felix is not here. And yet at the same time there are still feelings of happiness – this is a joyful time of year – but always with this undercurrent. I feel all out of sync.

28 December

Well, darling, we got through Christmas without you. A sort of numbness and disbelief descended again, like when you first died. I think it's because Christmas is so packed full of age-old ritual; we do things we've done year in, year out, all our lives. We go to Mass, put up lights, get a tree, eat mince pies. These traditions are like a stark frame that accentuates anything that is different, such as the glaring hole of your absence. It helped in a way. I was able to float through Christmas, going through the rituals in a sort of disconnected way; I felt distanced from it all, and from your death.

On Christmas morning Yaara and I had a swim in Ladies Pool. The water was pointy daggers, our limbs pricked by darts of cold. Alex and I went to Mass at the abbey, where the music was beautiful as usual and I wept quite a few times. We visited the Blessed Sacrament Chapel and thought back to your funeral there, when it was full of family and friends, and you in your shroud on the bier surrounded by candles. We then lit candles for you and Grandma. Then we went home and collected Lucian, and we all went to the Green Hill. Dad had found your wish list on *Amazon* and had bought you Hermione's wand from Harry Potter, which was on the list. We opened the present standing by your grave. I told you how much we loved and missed you, and the three of us stood together holding each other as the wind howled round us. We left two mince pies for you under your Christmas tree.

On Boxing Day, Dad and I went for a long and increasingly wet walk along the top of the Dart Gorge, eventually making our way down past Combestone Farm to the West Dart, where I swam in Queenie Pool. It was swollen and fast-moving, with tendrils of foam making curly patterns on the water's surface. As I took the plunge into the cold, I felt a sudden, visceral sense of *everything disappearing – a kind of rewinding, a spiralling-back of myself, like falling down a rabbit hole, moving back to an inexplicable sense of primitive connection with you. I felt a communion with you, a touching of your essence, back to when you were physically part of me, inside me as a seed. And yet at the same time I felt transformed into a non-physical being, a spirit. I lost myself.*

It is Twixtmas. I'm sitting watching TV one evening and I glance up at Felix's photograph. A great wave of grief hits me like a juggernaut. I howl and howl. It's simply unbearable. I don't know how I can keep going. I feel incredibly empty and profoundly bored and unengaged with everything. It's a kind of hard, cold feeling of indifference. A friend's house has flooded but I don't want to go and help.

New Year is looming and I'm struggling with it. The fact that a new year is about to begin just highlights the passing of time without Felix. The anniversary of his death is approaching too. It is all still as vivid and vital and dominant as when it happened nine months ago. No signs of it fading any time soon.

On New Year's Eve we go to Anna and her husband Mark's karaoke party, which turns out to be rather hilarious. Judy, Anna, Milla and I have a dance routine we've prepared, a special performance of 'I Will Survive' that we've choreographed and rehearsed for the last few weeks. It brings the house down. Then we all get very drunk and do karaoke all night. My star turn is 'Anarchy in the UK'. I really let off steam, which I definitely need to do. At midnight we all link arms and sing 'Auld Lang Syne', then everybody cries 'Happy New Year!' and I dissolve into tears.

Birthday and death day

20 January 2018

Oh my darling, I miss you so much, so terribly, terribly much, and I can't see that feeling ever lessening. I went to the Green Hill yesterday, and although it was a grey, blustery day, the sea looked sharper and brighter than I've ever seen it; it was a block of blue in the distance. As soon as I reached your grave, I wept. I brought you a little posy with the only hellebore in our garden, plus rosemary and lavender. Bringing you herbs is comforting. It feels like a nurturing thing to do. I then walked down to the fire pit and a beautiful buzzard took off in front of me, its brown-and-cream stripes flashing.

I feel your memory fading and that really hurts. I can see you in a great expanse of sea, gradually drowning while I look on from a boat on the surface. Slowly your face is sinking into oblivion. I can't stand it.

I have started having bereavement counselling on the phone. It's a free service provided by SUDEP Action. I have mixed feelings about it. I've always felt a bit uncomfortable about telling a stranger my private struggles, and in my heart I don't want to do it. However, I feel I should give it a try, in the interests of doing all I can to help myself. I suppose it might have some beneficial effect.

In the first session, we talk about sudden traumatic death and its effect: the actual physical and emotional impact of a shock like that – how it is not something I will ever get over, but it's something I can learn to accommodate in my life. We also talk about responses to great loss – how people react differently from each other. Some retreat into themselves, others actively want to raise money – to 'do' something to make it better. Then, in the second session, I effectively relive finding out Felix had died. I tell the counsellor what happened, in all the detail, experiencing the pain all over again, crying and shaking. I wonder if this is helpful? Perhaps if I actively try to relive what happened, it will eventually take the pain out of it? I don't know. I don't think doing this will give me any more insight or understanding than what I already have. Perhaps it is about desensitising?

February comes around. Alex and I head up to the Green Hill. We take daffodils for Felix. Afterwards we walk from the village nearby, Ashprington, down a green lane to Bow Creek, which runs off the Dart Estuary. As we get nearer to the water, the lane gets narrower, until it is a green tunnel. Wild garlic leaves are bursting forth at the side of the path, and then we see some wild daffodils – small, delicate yellow flowers. We reach the creek and there is young sea beet growing on the shore, its leaves bright-green, squeaky and shiny. It feels heartening, a sign that spring is on its way. And yet Felix is not here. It feels wrong, when new life is forming. I still can't get over the fact that his remains are buried nearby in a field. It seems surreal, impossible, wrong. His birthday is approaching and friends are asking if there's anything I'm planning. I just don't know. I don't know how I'll feel. The reality is that every day is pretty hellish and his birthday will be no different.

I have been wondering about what I can do to raise money for SUDEP Action. I feel the need to do this quite strongly. It will make me feel better to raise money for the cause, and also, if I organise some kind of event, it will be an opportunity to say Felix's name again, and do something in his memory. My pal Matt is a great one for thinking up catchy titles; ages ago, before Felix died, he came up with the title 'The Darty Dozen' – for a future event on Dartmoor, although he had no idea what such an event might be. We put our heads together and think. How about spending a weekend on Dartmoor and doing twelve swims in the process? We'll invite friends and they can each pay a tenner to take part. We'll limit numbers to fifty, to keep it manageable. But that will be £500 in one fell swoop. I start to plan, researching routes and swim spots, and looking into campsites.

At the same time, we are moving house. Things are getting busier. It seems hardly believable that we're leaving the house where Felix grew up. He lived here from the age of three, and somehow he grew up to be a man and I didn't even realise it had happened. And then he died. We are leaving because this house, although we love it, is a total headache and a financial drain. I have enough grief in my life with the loss of Felix, without added stress over the house. I feel as though I'm in a whirlwind. We have so much stuff to do. Getting things ship-shape, keeping the house in a constant state of tidiness for viewings, finances to arrange – it's a lot to deal with. But I feel it has to be done, for the sake of an easier, calmer, more peaceful life. At the same time, Felix's birthday is looming and I want to mark it and yet I don't. I don't know what to do.

15 February

My dearest, darling Felix, today you would have been twenty-one. It just doesn't bear thinking about. I feel utterly miserable and heartbroken. You were on the brink of your life, starting to adventure and explore, finding the courage you'd lacked before, and then bang: it all ends.

Facebook is reminding me to wish you Happy Birthday. Facebook doesn't know you're dead. It all seems laughable. In the end, I'm alone in my grief. Friends have been reaching out, sending their support, which means a lot, but there is nothing they can do. It helps to feel their love, but it doesn't change anything. Nothing changes the ghastly reality of your death, aged twenty.

I wish you Happy Birthday, my darling. You are my son – you always will be. You were born twenty-one years ago today – nothing changes that fact. You came into the world on 15 February 1997 and you left it on 9 March 2017. Not that the date really matters. You died. It's a hard fact, as hard as ice, as hard as granite, as hard as cold, raw, unforgiving winter. That is what your death feels like. I love you for ever.

We are snowbound. The worst snow for decades has gripped Devon and no one can go anywhere. Thousands of people across the country have been trapped in cars. A young girl has died. There is about 5 inches of snow and everything is held in a sort of soft silence. It feels historic. And I feel sad that Felix is not here to experience it with us, be part of it. He is not part of this event of late February and early March 2018, when the Beast from the East and Storm Emma collided to create a small snowmageddon.

I think back to snow in the past, in Felix and Lucian's childhood. I remember when Felix was about six and Lucian was about three, we had our first Dartmoor snow. We took the surfboards up to Saddle Tor, where we placed the boys on them and pushed them down the hill, to much excitement. They stood in the snow, Lucian toddling, tiny in the whiteness. I remember, before that, when Felix was about three, staying with my parents and making a snowman. In a photo, Felix stands beside the snowman grinning, in his yellow duffle coat. The snowman has stone eyes and a carrot nose, and is about double the size of him.

Just three weeks after Felix's birthday, it is the anniversary of his death. I visit the Green Hill on my own. It is a gloriously sunny early-spring day, a day in isolation from the dark dreary days around it. Kate has given me some snake's-head fritillary plants and I kneel down beside the grave and start to dig. Tarka lies quietly beside me as I make holes in the incredibly stony ground. Below me, the

tide is out, the river a winding line in the mud. After plant-
ing the fritillary, I tidy up and then lie down, snuggling up
to the mound of the grave. It feels good to be beside Felix,
in contact with the earth, with the sun warming my body.

I return the next day with Alex to a total contrast. It
pours with rain; it pours and pours. Alex places a daffodil
on the grave and we stand there for a short while, and I
start to cry, awful heaving-crying like being sick. We
retreat to the cob building and stand in the shelter looking
down at the river in the all-encompassing grey murk. We
are together, but still apart in our grief. But I am realising
that this does not matter. Alex has his grief, and I have
mine. We cannot somehow merge our experiences and
make things any easier. He has to mourn Felix in his own
way, which is private. I feel the need to talk about Felix,
to share my grief. Both ways are equally valid, and I have
to learn that my way is not his. The idea that we can share
our grief is a fantasy. We have to give each other space to
grieve, and unite to survive.

11 March

*It's Mother's Day again — the second since you died, and it feels
like being kicked when I'm down. I was up before Alex and
Lucian, as usual, and wandered around the house feeling desperate. I cried as I did the washing-up. Then I knocked over and
broke the 'Little Miss Sunshine' egg cup you gave me and burst
into tears all over again. Dad came down and stuck it back
together for me.*

*Later I cheered up a bit. It was pouring with rain again, but I
did a forensic weather analysis to try to work out the best place to*

walk, as we felt we just had to get out. We decided to do a walk from Kenton, based purely on the hope that it was the least likely place it would be raining. When we got there, hey presto, it was dry, and we walked through the Powderham Estate, with its herds of deer, to the Exe Estuary. We saw lots of birds — long-tailed tits, chaffinches, crows, Canada geese, moorhens, mallards, coots, oystercatchers, sanderlings, redshanks, herons and last, and most magnificently, curlews. They were spectacular, wading around in the marshes on their long, elegant legs, with their curved spiked beaks and warbling, mournful cries.

I'm having frequent flashbacks while driving. They often seem to happen in the car. Suddenly my mind is full of moments from the discovery of Felix's death and its aftermath. Being inside the ambulance. Sitting in the wood-panelled room waiting for the police. Seeing his body in the open coffin at the undertakers, his face black, but so childlike.

Today my father is ninety-three. It is such a great age but it feels out of kilter with Felix's death at just twenty. In bed, I find it hard to sleep, and toss and turn, unable to settle. Eventually I go to Felix's room and sleep there. On waking, I feel a desperate need to immerse myself in the sea.

I meet a swimming pal, Ju, for a swim at Hopes Nose in Torquay. We walk down the path to the limestone prom-ontory that sticks out into the sea. There are a couple of guys fishing. It is low water and a beautiful little beach is exposed on the northern side of the headland, packed with grey pebbles and rocks, many striped with seams of pink-and-white twinkly quartz. The sea is calm and clasps us in its coldness. I feel a closeness to Felix in the sea. I feel small in the vastness, and I feel a loss of self. I am more like a spirit, an essence, which is what he is now. My body is weightless, insignificant. I'm just the essence of me, and yet I feel I am not me; I am nothing. I am in some sort of ephemeral existence. I am losing myself.

I have a couple more sessions of the phone counselling but then I stop. I just feel I am reliving the pain all over again. It works for lots of people, but not for me.

The weather is mad. We're now having a mini-heatwave, just a month after heavy snow. Crazy weather, but at long last it feels as though we have come out of the endless, endless winter. In the last few weeks I have started to feel a little more positive about life. A year has passed since Felix died, and summer is coming.

Year Two

A gathering on Dartmoor

3 April 2018

My darling Felix, last night I found myself looking at your Facebook page again and reading all the hundreds of shocked and heartfelt comments made by people on hearing the news. I cried and cried. This is not actually a bad thing. I want to cry; I want to continue to feel the reality of your death. As your death moves further away in time, I want it to continue to feel harsh, raw, real. If it fades, you fade. Death is now part of your identity. It's something I have to embrace, to live with. The pain is part of you and my continuing relationship with you.

It is the anniversary of Grandma's death. She died five years ago this week. I feel so differently about her death. I am over it, in a way I will never be 'over' yours. It was in the natural order of things. I miss her, of course, but not in the same way I miss you. It is fine for her to fade. The wound of your loss is like a hole left by a tooth that has been wrenched out. It will never heal and the hole will always be there.

As I embark on my second year without Felix, I think about time. The completion of a year without him seems significant, and I suppose it is, because we measure our lives in time. It is a way of deriving meaning, of trying to understand and make sense of our existence. By marking anniversaries, we can compare years with one another, think about what has changed, and whether it is for better or worse.

I have got through my first year without Felix. And as the second begins, I am wondering how it will play out. Felix died in early spring, when new life was unfurling. And now, a year later, the cycle is starting again. Primroses, daffodils and tulips are springing out of the ground. This is, of course, a stark contrast to the deadness of Felix. But I am glad the anniversary occurs at this time. The new growth reminds me that life continues, and is circular.

It's the Friday night of the early May bank holiday weekend, and we're sitting in the Forest Inn, a fairly basic pub pretty much in the middle of Dartmoor. We're with friends, eating pizza, having pitched camp at Huccaby Farm down the road, which has a field bordering the West Dart. The river makes a huge bend just here, with a large oval pool where you can swim. It is an idyllic spot, with a tap and some loos, and that's about it. Eight years ago, we had Alex's fortieth birthday celebrations here, with a campfire, silent films and silent disco. Family and friends came, and we were blessed with lovely weather.

A gathering on Dartmoor

We are here again with friends, and again the weather is being kind to us. Although it's only early May, it's hot. This time we are gathering for the Darty Dozen – twelve swims over two days on Dartmoor – to celebrate Felix and raise money for SUDEP Action. Everyone has paid a tenner to take part, and I've devised a weekend of walks with swims. As we amble, slightly drunk, back down the lane to the campsite in the gathering darkness, I feel cheered by the thought of the weekend ahead. Friends are close by; we will be up and about tomorrow, and hiking through the vast, beloved expanse of Dartmoor, actively remembering, layering today on everything that has come before – including Felix's life, and times when he himself was here in this bucolic spot by the river.

The next morning, we drive to Princetown for the first walk and swim of the weekend. The village has rather a lot of grey, slightly depressing buildings. It always feels somehow devoid of life, spirit. HMP Dartmoor dominates life here, and that is probably why. Physically, its dark form looms, and is visible from pretty much every point around. The village is out of keeping with its setting. By rights there should not be a place of this size here.

In the car park, everyone greets each other excitedly, and I hand out orange SUDEP Action T-shirts. There are around fifty of us, so we make quite a colourful crowd. We set off down 'Conchies Road', so called after the conscientious objectors during the First World War, who built it as part of their sentence of hard labour. About a thousand of them were sent to Dartmoor Prison after refusing to fight. Conchies Road is a wide track that heads south from Princetown, and we walk in the heat into a great parched landscape spreading as far as the eye can see.

This part of the moor is quite featureless, but imposing and impressive in its emptiness. We pass South Hessary Tor, and then reach Devonport Leat, a small, man-made waterway that was built more than 200 years ago to supply fresh drinking water to Plymouth. Our orange column paces beside it. The water is clear, with tiny fish darting about among bright-green weed that flows in long swathes, reminding me of the famous painting of Ophelia by John Everett Millais. After a while, we head away from the leat to find Crazywell Pool, our first swim spot. A huge, lozenge-shaped lake, a relic of tin mining, it sits in a dip, so you can't see it until you're right on top of it. There are gasps from those who haven't been here before when they catch sight of it. It is grand, spectacular and inviting. We plunge in, and it is such a joy to see the water full of people, all here because of Felix, smiling and laughing. I swim to one end and quietly lay a boulder on the bottom, remembering my beautiful son, wishing he was here.

The next swim is a total contrast. Black Tor Falls is a small waterfall with a little pool, overhung by a tree in a little dell. It's a bit like 'How many people can you fit in a Mini?' There's much hilarity as we all try to pack in, some shrieking under the cascading water, some sitting on the side, cooling their feet, and others wallowing. We take turns to sit under the crashing water as there's only room for a couple at a time. We sit and have lunch in the blazing sun, and then set off for the final swim of the day, at Foggintor Quarry. We stand at the edge, looking down on a huge hole in the ground filled with water, surrounded by great grey cliffs, with a couple of tufty islands in the middle. I remember coming here in the dead of winter with Alex and the boys. Thick icicles hung from the cliff walls and the pool was frozen; the boys threw stones on it that skidded across the ice. Now, a decade or so on, we are here again in such different circumstances. We fill the place and, once again, I feel happy and glad.

The next day we walk down the River Dart from Dartmeet, through ancient, shady oak woods, clambering over mossy boulders and stopping for numerous swims. As we get deeper into the gorge, the river is bordered by vast lumps of granite, which heat up in the sun. At Broada Stones — just about the middle, and most remote part, of the gorge — we lie on the roasting slabs and swim in the pools and waterfalls, before fording the river, rucksacks balanced on heads, in what feels like an almost biblical crossing. On the other side of the river, we hike back up to Dartmeet, swimming in Venford Falls and, finally, in Queenie Pool on the West Dart, a quiet and beautiful oval of delicious, clear water.

Being with these people, some of whom are really good friends, while others I have only just met for the first time, I feel a sense of closeness and companionship, an unspoken connection over Felix, who not everyone knew. It is a connection from our common humanity and from our love — our love for our children and for each other, our fragility highlighted by Felix's death. I hope this weekend will become a tradition, and that it will be something positive out of what has happened. And perhaps in future it will be a way for us to honour, celebrate and remember other loved ones who have died.

A few days later, after I've recovered from the exhaustion and excitement of the weekend, when I was frankly on a bit of a high, I go for a walk on my own down the Yellow Brick Road to the Dart. Tarka skips ahead, and the wind cuts across us as we walk across the top of the moor and past my favourite hut circle. As we start to descend to the river, there are little blasts of sunlight as the sun tries to break through. Approaching the valley that goes down to the water, I see little touches of blue, but the bluebells are not really out yet; they must be late this year because of the extended winter. I head down through the valley to the bottom, where I stand at the top of the cliff overlooking Black Pool and look across to Luckey Tor on the opposite bank; it is the only tor on Dartmoor that is at river level. It sits solidly on the ground, rising up like a castle keep, partially hidden by dazzling vegetation. The trees in front of it are bursting into bud, in a million shades of green. I sit on a mossy bank under a tree and look at the river below, a mass of rocks and white water. I am all too aware that a year has passed since Felix died, and I feel I must be active to stop him fading. I decide to try to speak to him out loud. To tell him about the weekend and what a wild success it was. But I can't keep up the talking for long. It doesn't feel right. Surely I should be able to talk to him, to sit and think about him for a long while, to devote my mind and thoughts to him? But I can't. I think it brings me up against the harsh reality of his absence, and is just too much to deal with.

15 June

I am sitting on a deck chair in an empty room in our new house. We are moving from the home where you grew up, which feels like the right thing to do, but obviously it is a wrench at the same time. *We're not moving because you died. We wanted to move anyway – the house is costly to maintain – but it is a distraction, too, to have a new house to work on. I do really need that distraction, as I am really fighting total gloom at the moment; my spirits have sunk very low and I feel it is impossible to lift them. I just cannot accept your death; I really can't. I'll never be able to, and that level of pain and loss just feels impossible to deal with – it's just too much. I do think a lot about dying – what a release that would be. I assume it would release me from the pain but perhaps that wouldn't actually be the case. Perhaps I might be reunited with you. Who knows?*

I'm finding it very difficult to find energy from anywhere to keep going. Luckily, we have been having a spell of good weather so I've been swimming virtually every day. The river is warm and lush, and I have been offering lots of boulders for you; the water is warm enough to dive and submerge completely, and that is a tremendous balm, being consumed by the water, feeling myself sink below the surface. I love to swim underwater among the rocky outcrops, the beds of rock, the boulders, some lined with dark-green moss, others velvety with silt.

I had a wonderful sea swim with my pal Matt a few days ago. We took the Cliff Railway down to Oddicombe Beach in Torquay as the sun beat down. We swam north along the coast and to the entrance of the Juliet Cave but it was too rough to enter. Do you remember the time, a few years ago, when we discovered that cave? I remember telling you about it, as I was so thrilled. Matt and I were swimming along the coastline when we saw a large, dark opening in the cliffs. As we approached it, we saw another, higher hole to the left of the main opening. As we got nearer, we realised we could climb up a smooth slope of pink rock to the higher hole. At the top of it we found an extraordinary round pool containing lots of pretty pebbles, like an 'upstairs' with a 'window' or 'balcony' looking down onto the cave next door. And so it was christened the 'Juliet Cave'.

As Matt and I swam, the sea was very sparkly and warm. On we went past the old quarry, a magnificent buttress against the sea, and along to Petit Tor, where we saw a nudist sitting near some bushes. As we swam back, we had to push a bit. There was an incoming tide that was moving north up the coast; we were heading back south. It felt good to be distracted in the sea, held by the salty expanse, lost in the aquatic world. I definitely feel a connection to you here – a sort of elemental link.

I feel great pressure to get myself out of this low, partly because I know what it's like when it gets really bad – how incapacitated it can make me – and I don't want that. It feels different from other periods of depression in my life because this is the worst thing that has ever happened to me and I can't imagine anything else happening that could be worse. So, in a sense, there is more pressure to do something, as this is a life-long thing; I am going to have to live with your death for the rest of my life.

It's a balancing act between trying to keep going and 'giving in to it', not that 'giving in to it' is the right phrase – more like 'going with it', perhaps. If I resist and resist, I know I will end up crashing badly, breaking down because it will come out one way or another. But if I can acknowledge and allow it, perhaps it is like releasing a valve, in a controlled way; I can depressurise, decompress. It's all about trying to manage it, and I do know what I need to do: keep swimming, don't work too much, cuddle the dog . . . but sometimes it is all just too much and that's where I am at the moment. I just have to hang on in there and, somehow, get through.

We are having the most amazing heatwave, with temperatures of around 27 degrees. It's been going on for more than a week. Devon is utterly beautiful – green, lush and soaked in sun. I have been in the Dart every day, submerging in its depths, seeking refuge from the heat. I like swimming underwater best, moving amid a kaleidoscope of dynamic sunlight, sunbeams bouncing down to the river bed and up again.

I have been working with friends Nick and Michele on their cookery book in the evenings. Driving back home afterwards, I have seen the most stunning panorama of English countryside every night: fields and hills in greens and yellows, bathed in fading light. One night, the sun was setting and the shadows were long, and I just felt such an ache of sadness that Felix is not here to experience this beauty. Somehow, beauty makes his loss so much more intense, and just seeing beauty triggers the pain of his loss – knowing that he is not there to be part of it and to experience it.

The heatwave continues. People are already talking about the historic summer of 2018. It really is quite extraordinary, quite unlike an English summer. There is persistent sunshine and warmth, and every day is the same; it is just unheard of. Again, these 'historic' happenings emphasise Felix's absence.

30 June

Darling Felix, I visited you today about 6 p.m. There was no one around. I didn't have flowers with me so I made a posy from all the flowers growing at the Green Hill: ox-eye daisies, hawkbit, red campion, kidney vetch, yarrow and clover. I love these wild flowers, which take me back to my childhood, when I learned their names and used to press them and put them in books. I remember trying to teach you and Lucian the names of flowers and trees but I don't know how much you retained. I suspect you were never very interested.

At your graveside I saw that some love-in-the-mist has self-seeded right next to your headstone. It is a delicate blue. This heartened me so much: a physical manifestation of love continuing.

I squatted down by your grave and put my face in the grasses. I saw a tiny brown moth perched on a stem. Then a ladybird crawling up a stalk. Then a fly. All quietly there in the silence of the burial ground. Your grave supports all this life and growth. I felt a world apart, separate, in time and place, with my face among the plants and animals on your grave, with you, with life, death, existence, mortality itself.

Sean comes with his husband Steve to visit. We go up to the Green Hill, where the grass is brown, parched by the heat. Walking into the meadow, I still have a sense of utter disbelief that what remains of Felix's body is lying underground. I wonder about the state of his body now. Is it down to bones, perhaps? Although the flesh might have gone, the bones will remain there for many years – hundreds of years, possibly. But that is no comfort. Was Felix his body anyway? Perhaps his body is all he was.

Sean, Steve and I sit down by Felix's grave and talk, sweltering in the shadeless heat. Usually there is wind up here but today it is completely still. We talk about the fear of losing our memories of Felix, of him fading away. A lot of grief advice now is about 'keeping the relationship going' by talking about the person, thinking about them, writing about them, creating rituals for them. But sometimes I wonder is this actually helpful? The reality is that Felix is *dead*. Maybe I just need to accept that – accept that the memories will fade, that he is gone and he won't come back.

28 July

Darling, we have moved house but it's all gone wrong. There is a leak in one of the rooms and we are stuck in limbo while the plumbers try to work out what is going on. I feel so unsettled and stuck; we have been so busy and exhausted with the move, there hasn't been time for you. I don't feel I have a home.

I have been feeling remarkably unemotional about leaving our home of nearly twenty years, where we brought you up and where so much happened. Now, though, I think it's starting to hit me, the sense of being rootless, homeless. The problem is I can't settle in our new home yet. We haven't even got our own bed.

You don't have a 'place' in the new house; you were never here. That is obviously an omission, a problem, and yet we couldn't have stayed in our old home for ever. I will have to work out what to do about that. Do I need some sort of shrine?

If you were alive, you would just have finished your second year at university. I wonder what you would be doing now? More plays, I expect, and films, probably, too. I feel so proud of the way you faced your fears, your shyness, your epilepsy, in getting involved with acting. What an amazing human being you were.

Our annual Cornish holiday comes around again. It's the second without Felix and there is such an enormous gap where he should be. Like last year, I bring a framed photo and we bring him treasures every day. On the first day, on my first swim, I find a skeleton of a sea potato, which I feel is a good omen as I didn't manage to find one last year. It is beautiful – mathematical in its precise beauty, heart-shaped and pierced with rows of tiny holes.

That night I stand on the balcony and look out on Gillan Creek and further out to the horizon. Boats are motionless in the water, the light is constantly changing. It is a timeless scene, where Felix should be, but he isn't. My brother Ned and I swim out to the Herra, the little headland at the mouth of the creek, where there are the remains of a prehistoric cliff castle. It is easy going out, but tough coming back against the wind. With every stroke, I think of Felix, my face in the water looking down at the shell-studded sand below.

Two days into the holiday, my father, who is ninety-three, has a spectacular fall and gashes his head. He has several wounds and is even more fragile than before. We take it in turns to do night shifts, to try to prevent any more accidents. When it's my turn, I either sleep in his bed with him or on the sofa next door. It is all very exhausting and I get more and more tired. My eczema flares up and when we finally get home from the holiday, I feel as though I need another one to recover.

Round the island again

10 September

Oh Felix, I miss you so terribly much; there's a kind of splinter in my heart. It's like Kai in the Snow Queen story: I have been changed by your death, and not for the better. There is a sort of hard selfishness deep inside that wasn't there before. I think it must be about survival and self-preservation, about not being so beholden to other people — frankly, not caring about their worries any more — because your death has hurt me, changed me so utterly. I am not angry, just hard — deeply damaged, I think — and I need to be selfish to survive.

Yet there is still joy. Yesterday, I had joy in bucketloads. We swam around Burgh Island, following my September birthday tradition, in really quite fearsome conditions, with towering waves slapping us down and bouncing us back and forth. There were strong south-westerlies so we decided to go anti-clockwise to get the toughest bit over first. I honestly didn't think we would do it — we took ages to get anywhere — but the sun was bright and glistening on the waves and there was dramatic foam on the rocks — quite beautiful. We just kept going, slowly. Eventually we got to the first corner at the back and suddenly it got easier; there was still a great swell but we were being pushed the right way. We swam alongside the enormous, stark slate cliff with its rows of sharp, dark pinnacles, and saw Death Valley awaiting up ahead. This is a chasm-like gulley you can swim through at the back of the island. We bounced through and out into an eddy that threatened to throw us onto the rocks. We swam strongly out of the eddy, and then stopped to admire a row of cormorants silhouetted against the setting sun, lined up like aquatic meerkats. And all the time we had Lucian and our friend Rob accompanying us in kayaks, for which we were very glad. You should have been with us in a kayak, too.

We went round the final side of the island with the wind pushing us, past the Mermaid Pool, and then swam across the causeway (it was high water), which was also pretty tough as the current was pushing us the other way, towards Bantham. Finally, we reached the shore, and oh, the euphoria! We were on a massive high. Everyone was grinning like Cheshire cats, it felt so good, and I also felt so blessed to have these friends that I have been swimming with for at least a decade now. It felt like old times, like before you died; we were always there in September doing this swim, on my birthday. There have been years of gathering below the rocks, swimming the island, picnicking, barbecuing. It's one of those regular points in my life, so the fact you weren't there was incredibly tough and always will be. And yet these familiar moments in my year provide vital continuity, while at the same time emphasising your absence.

Lucian and I are off to Sheffield to check out the university. He's accepted a place to study computer science but hasn't actually been there. We arrive late on the Friday night and head out to the nearest pub to find some supper. We walk in and are immediately surrounded by young people. It's a real student pub – lots of noise, laughter, people wearing DMs. I haven't been in a pub like this for years. The pubs I go to in Devon are usually quiet and full of middle-aged and old people. It makes me quite emotional; it reminds me so much of when I was a student back in the 1980s, having intense conversations in pubs, and of course it reminds me of Felix, and his life as a student at Leicester – those formative years as a young adult, first going out into the world, living away from home, meeting new people, learning about life beyond your immediate experience.

The next day we visit various halls of residence, and Lucian goes off to see the labs and departmental facilities. All in all, we love Sheffield, and Lucian feels enthused by the idea of going there. We come back feeling positive.

The next day, though, I feel very emotional. Seeking comfort, I go to Mass at the abbey, but can barely hold back the tears. I sit in the car afterwards, crying uncontrollably, shaking. It must be a reaction to the Sheffield visit, which, while a great success, was also a huge trigger for thinking about Felix and his student days, and finding him dead in his hall of residence. After, I go to the Green Hill, but I just feel empty.

The Green Hill

30 October

Oh darling, I am lying here with the most revolting swollen, bruised leg like a member of a Victorian freak show. A large area above my right knee is a hideous deep-purple colour. I was setting up my latest SUDEP fundraising event, when a piece of staging fell on me. I feel lucky to be alive, to be honest. What if it had fallen on my head? The only consolation is that, by some miracle, I haven't broken anything.

It's weird: it makes me feel kind of doomed, like I attract trouble and problems. I wonder somehow if your death has made me weaker, more susceptible to accidents and illness? I think there is some truth in this — I was reading about it recently. Terrible bereavement must inevitably weaken one's defences.

I am writing to Felix less frequently. It's hard to accept, but I don't feel quite such a desperate urge to write as I did when he first died. This doesn't mean the pain is lessening, but perhaps I am feeling it in a different way. I am getting used to it. It is a bit like carrying a heavy backpack. At first it is really hard and you feel the weight of it all the time. Gradually, though, you get stronger and can cope better with the burden. You get used to carrying it around all the time.

I can't help but notice that the reduction in my letters to him started with the beginning of the second year since he died. It makes me wonder about time. Days, weeks, months, years seem like arbitrary divisions of time, designed to organise and carve up life. But perhaps they do mark significant periods. The intensity of feeling in the year after Felix died could not have continued.

13 November

I miss you so very much and I'm feeling as though it's getting worse, not better. It's eighteen months since you died, and on one level it is sort of 'normal' now, the fact of your death, but on another it is not, it is still gross, unbelievable. I walk past photographs of you every day in the house — you are there, that is what you are now: a photograph, a memory. I am torn between trying to accept that and at the same time refusing, unable to accept that.

Lucian is off to Lapland soon to work as a kitchen porter in one of the resorts. I am worrying a lot about this; worrying about him being safe. He slept in very late this morning, and while I was waiting for him to get up, I even started to fear he might have died in his sleep in the night. These feelings are real. They do not help. But they are there.

It's hard to keep caring about life sometimes. Sometimes I just want to forget it all, and other times, quite frequently actually, I wake up in the night with a terrible sense of fear, of horror, of darkness, and I have to tell myself not to worry; to rise above it. But it doesn't take away the feeling of fear that took over in the first place.

This is such a dead time of year. In the run-up to Christmas, I have work to distract me but I hate the short days and the darkness. It has suddenly hit me how Felix's death has changed my whole mental landscape, the operation of my mind, and my thoughts. I am realising that I think about him all the time, pretty much every minute of every day. This profoundly affects my life. Never before has one subject ever taken over totally and permanently like this. In some way it is a bizarre comfort: Felix is with me more comprehensively in my thoughts, at least, than ever he was before. If he hadn't died, he wouldn't be crowding my mind like this.

I still feel a sense of disbelief that he is not here. It's so shocking. One night I decide to look at his Facebook page. It is kind of comforting. I'm pretending he's still here in the same way that everybody else is. Then I look at our conversation on Messenger. I even 'wave' at him. I'm thankful for our digital, social-media age; there are many traces to revisit and it does help to do this, as if I am spending some time with Felix again.

I still often think of his actual body, decaying in the ground at the Green Hill. When we saw his body when it was brought back from Leicester, I remember Alex said to me, 'Felix isn't there; his spirit is gone.' But I feel, and still do, a profound connection with his physical body, because it's what I always related to. Holding him, cuddling him, feeling him near. When I think of his body rotting underground, well, I find it hard to think of the decomposition and decay, his flesh disappearing, only his bones remaining – but that skeleton is still him, and it is still there. As for his spirit, well, I don't know about that. He will always live in my mind, as part of me, but whether he is still in existence in another form, I just do not know.

My father is in a bad way. He has Lewy body dementia and has been declining rapidly in the last few months. He's gone from being quite frail but fairly on the ball to extremely frail and unable to do things like dress himself or walk across the room without falling over. For the last four years he has been living with Kate and Ned, who have looked after him so beautifully. But now it is getting more and more difficult for them to cope. When the community nursing team start talking about the need for a hoist, we realise, shockingly, that Dad will have to go into a home. It is just heart-breaking. Ned and Kate find one fairly nearby, in Aylesbury, and I go to visit a few days after he moves in. It is about three weeks before Christmas. It is a modern and well-equipped home but it just feels utterly depressing. It is big and anonymous, and full of people we don't know. God's waiting room. Dad is so weak.

Two days before Christmas, I visit again. Dad is lying in bed, his eyes closed, his mouth open. I hold his hand and there is the faintest, momentary opening of his eyes, before they shut again. I talk to him and he doesn't respond. Tarka is with me and I lift her furry face up to his. He doesn't respond.

I look at the books by his bedside. A small, worn, brown hardback lies there: *Trout of the Thames* by A. E. Hobbs. I pick up the little book, published in 1947, when Dad was twenty-two. Chapter headings include 'A trout fisher is born', 'A less typical day', 'Otters and Trout' and 'My most exciting catch'. I start to read the book to him out loud, and am taken back to scenes from my childhood: fishing with Dad on the Thames at Marlow; him getting absolutely infuriated with me when I couldn't get the hang of casting; long car journeys punctuated by huge detours to find bodies of water to stop next to and observe fish. As I read, Dad continues to lie there, unresponsive. I stay for about an hour and then leave.

Christmas number two

Christmas Day

Happy Christmas, darling Felix — our second without you. We did the same this year as last. I went for a swim in the Dart at Spitch-wick first thing and then we went to the abbey. It was a beautiful mass with heavenly singing, as usual, and I mostly kept it together, with just the odd little weep. Then Dad, Uncle Matthew and I went to the Green Hill, where the sun was pushing through behind the graves but ahead the hills and the river were wreathed with mist. Your small Christmas tree that I placed there a couple of weeks ago looked perfect — not bedraggled by all the rain, as I had feared. Dad had brought a lantern and we lit a candle. Kate had sent you a present, which we put on your headstone for a bit. Then we opened it, and it was three Christmas decorations: one a beautiful wooden F; the others two Harry Potter *decorations. Perfect. We put them on the tree. It gave me an idea. I'm going to buy a new Christmas decoration for you every year from now on. It will be your Christmas present. I had a little cry and then we went home. Yaara arrived and we had a beautiful meal, and now the day is over for another year.*

Two days after Christmas, I get a phone call from Ned. Dad has died. He died overnight in the nursing home. Ned had seen him the day before. I feel utterly distraught at the thought of him dying alone, but at least he was only in the home for a few weeks, and in truth, judging by the last time I saw him, I don't think he knew any longer what was going on. So, now he, Mum and Felix are gone. All in the space of five years. So much love has disappeared from my life.

In a bizarre way I am 'coping'. I am working; I am not crying all the time. But I have had some big crying attacks that have taken me by surprise. I've gone back to that heaving, undignified howling that happened a lot when Felix first died.

Recently I read something a bereaved parent wrote. 'Bereaved parents quickly learn to deceive.' It's very true. To keep going, you behave normally; and on one level, as a result, normality seems to return. But that is a deception. I think there is also a learning process – learning to deal with the grief, which involves both self-deception and the deception of others. It's one of the things you learn in order to keep going. A necessary evil.

The Green Hill

15 February 2019

Dear Felix

Today you would have been twenty-two. Last night Dad and I watched the video of your life again that Dad put together after you died. I cried uncontrollably. I sat there on the sofa, the TV screen filled with you, hardly able to see it through my tears. There you were, a toddler, giggling and eating yoghurt in your high chair. Then, aged about seven, with Lucian, riding your bikes around the drive. A little older, rock-pooling unenthusiastically in France. And then, a kind of postscript, a video made by you when you were about sixteen. You speak directly to the camera, your face filling the screen, and start with a close-up of you cleaning your teeth, the beginnings of a moustache forming above your lip. Then there are wobbly shots of your very messy bedroom. And a voiceover.

'Hmm. Well. This is my room. Saturday . . . no . . . yes, Saturday 12th. Dad's here. Mum's gone off to see her friend Giovanna. We're about to head to the beach. It's a lovely sunny day.'

Then the video cuts to the outside of the house. Sunbeams fill the screen, obscuring everything else. The camera turns towards the house.

'There's our house. Let's see if I can get further back. It's a very big house; I can't get it all in. Here is the garden . . . There's a nice little path . . . It's very, very bright. Here's a very strange sculpture my dad made . . . He's an artist, a good one at that. Mmm. So, here we are back in the car. Off to the beach. Bantham. It's a very nice place.'

Oh, the sound of your voice, the gentleness of your voice, your awkwardness, your presence on the TV screen. How strange and beautiful, yet eerie, too.

This morning I went to the Green Hill. It was an unseasonably beautiful day, with the meadow bathed in strong sun while larks sang overhead. I was hoping the miniature daffodils I planted a few months ago would be showing but they weren't. I lay down by your grave and the sun kissed my face. It really was beautiful. I had brought you some daffodils tied together with an ivy frond. Then I took a walk down the field and visited Lynne, my dear friend who died of cancer in 2016. She was such a fan of yours, always making the effort to talk to you, and asking after you when you weren't there. She would have been utterly devastated by your death. I walked back and spent some more time with you. Then I went down to the river, where it felt uncannily like spring. As I walked along the bank, I was surrounded by tiny shoots of wild garlic coming through, fresh and green. The sky was blue and the river silky, benign and still. Geese honked overhead, all the sounds crystal clear because of the lack of wind. I swam towards you, as I always do, looking up at the graveyard.

A few days later, I visit the Green Hill again. It's mid-afternoon and the sun is behind me, setting, but the meadow is still – just – in the sun. I can hear crows squawking overhead, and in front of me is the river, which is quite low; it's a spring tide and there's a large expanse of viscous-looking mud. I think of Felix down below in the earth, and his degrading body, his remains. There are some pale green points pushing up out of his grave. I can hear lambs bleating on the nearby hillside. The daffodils I laid on his headstone last time are still looking really lovely.

I think about Felix in the video, about sixteen years old, recording his life as it unfolded one Saturday morning, a Saturday morning like any other, heading off to the beach for some bodyboarding, the sun blasting into the camera, his young voice telling the viewer about his home and his life. Like a ghost in a machine, he is now thousands of animated pixels on a screen. Yet having him on film helps to keep a version of him alive. It is also, though, a painful thing to confront, as it highlights the stark reality of his absence and death. But that painful confrontation is something I feel is necessary to experience from time to time. I want to be able to seek it out, and so, on balance, I am glad we have these videos, which are a route back into the past.

Fear. That's something I'm increasingly aware of. Alex and I were sitting in the car yesterday, about to take Tarka for a walk. The rain was pouring down. I suddenly felt gripped by a fear in my heart, a generalised sense of fear, and of feeling insecure and out of place. I never used to have feelings like this. These feelings are getting more frequent. I wouldn't describe them as panic attacks, more like fear sensations.

As February turns to March, Yaara, Anna and I head to Argyll to stay with Anna's old friends Charlotte and Dougie. It's our third visit to this beautiful part of Scotland, with its crinkly coastline full of sea lochs, islands and woods. Charlotte and Dougie live in Carsaig Bay, overlooking the island of Jura, and on previous trips we have had a sort of *Swallows and Amazons*-type existence, going out on adventures in boats, swimming and snorkelling, and walking.

On this visit, the weather is quite the windiest and wildest it's ever been. Our first outing is to a loch at Scotnish, to do some snorkelling. The weather is truly ferocious – in fact we feel quite ridiculous standing on the side of the loch, trying to change into our wetsuits, being buffeted by the wind and lashed by rain. We end up howling with laughter as the whole thing seems absurd. Eventually, we are ready, and put our stuff under our coats in a vain attempt to keep it dry. We get in and the water is freezing. Privately, we wonder how on earth we are going to stick our faces into the water to snorkel, after a winter spent keeping our heads out of the water because of the cold. But as soon as we glimpse what is underneath us, the cold is forgotten and we are totally absorbed by the beauty and serenity below. Thousands, if not millions, of spindly brittle stars litter the loch bed, brilliantly black and fragile. It is like looking at an underwater universe. There are all manner of shells, and I also see what I later discover is an orange sea squirt, attached to a rock. Underwater, it looks like an orange condom gently moving, full of water, but when I take it out to have a look, it is like a fat sea slug, about the size of my thumb. The cold, wind and rain are forgotten as we swim with our heads down over a sea-grass meadow where the blades of grass are a crazy-bright green against the inky darkness of the brittle stars.

The second anniversary of Felix's death falls while I am in Scotland. I feel the kindness and warmth of my friends. On previous visits here, he was still alive. Yaara and I create a little shrine in the kitchen, made out of shells we gathered at Scotnish. We light a candle at breakfast. I feel strangely in control. Perhaps because I am away from home?

Year Three

The old stones

4 April 2019

My darling, I've just woken from a beautiful dream in which I had you back. It was so delicious that I felt utterly despairing when I woke up and realised it was just a dream. Nonsensically, I was back at my old, hated school, but as a parent, collecting you, the pupil. I waited and then you emerged with the others and I held you in my arms for what seemed like an age. Then everything was flooded with water and I'm not sure what happened to us after that. The overwhelming feeling of the dream was our closeness, our joy at being together – just being there together physically. That feeling of holding you, of cuddling you – that irreplaceable feeling. But also a feeling of drowning, drowning in love and drowning in death.

It's now just over two years since you've gone. When I look back at when you first died, it was all so surreal, living through the pain minute by minute, hour by hour, day by day in a sort of agonising intensity. Now it's a case of facing a life stretching out with, it seems, no hope of a lessening of the pain, which is dull and heavy, punctuated by sharp stabbings of hurt. Still the dissonance continues, the 'normality' of life carrying on and my feelings going on inside.

I had my annual review at work. There I was in the newsroom, working away efficiently, chatting, doing what I do, laughing with colleagues. Then I was in with my lovely boss James, who asked me how I was, and instantly I was in floods of tears, falling apart, a blubbering heap. It's this double life: it is so destabilising and makes me feel very insecure, as though I'm walking on a tightrope. My sadness feels like a very heavy weight that I cannot shift.

We are meeting our friends Benj and Neal over on 'The Dark Side' – the western side of Dartmoor, so–called as it usually gets all the worst of the weather. I want to visit the Langstone Moor stone circle, which I've seen pictured in an old black-and-white photo in an online collection of historic images of the moor. The collection is called the Dartmoor Archive and is a treasure trove of fascinating pictures of the past.

The stone circle is near Great Mis Tor and was restored in the last decade of the nineteenth century (when the photo was taken) by the Dartmoor Exploration Committee, a group of gentlemen antiquarians. I say 'restored' – what they did was re-erect the stones, which were all lying down.

There's something I find utterly compelling about the stone circles and rows, and the other ancient remains, in this part of Devon. They are so solid, unknowable, mysterious and still. I love their presence and their silence.

Dartmoor is packed with them, with over 1,500 burial cairns, more than 5,000 hut circles (the stone remains of thatched roundhouses), and over seventy stone rows. There are fewer stone circles; the generally accepted number is sixteen, though accounts vary. Many of the cairns contain human remains, often in a kist, a stone casket in which the ashes of the person were placed. The hut circles were for living in, and cairns and kists were for burying the dead. But as for the stone circles and rows, who knows why they were built? Could they have been for ceremonies, were they monuments to those who had died, or could they have been for worship? Something deep and primitive, enigmatic, draws me to them, especially after the loss of Felix.

We park at Smeardon Down near Peter Tavy and start a gradual ascent heading east. The sun is out and we get warm. We pass Stephen's Grave, a small stone marker like a miniature standing stone. It is a memorial to someone who died by their own hand; those who took their own lives were traditionally buried outside the parish boundary.

I think about one of our last-ever walks as a family, when Felix was still alive, in March 2016. We used to go on regular expeditions to look at Dartmoor's Bronze Age places. On this occasion, we set out to visit the Down Tor stone row on the southern side of the moor. It was one of those early spring days when you finally feel a sense of hope after the long winter. We climbed up Down Tor in the sunshine, scrambling over the boulders and clitter, and stood on the top, admiring the views down to Plymouth Sound. From there we descended the other side to try to find the stone row. It was an amazingly clear day, and soon the stone row came into view. It was the longest and straightest I'd ever seen, with a small but perfectly formed cairn circle at one end. It was like a mirage, stretching out in front of us, the stones almost floating in a seemingly never-ending line. We walked the full length, trying – and failing – to count the stones. We didn't think much about what we were doing at the time, but now, looking back, that walk takes on much greater significance. We were walking among a graveyard of memory, made by our ancestors from hundreds of generations ago, and now, two years on from Felix's death, here I am again, searching out another place that speaks of memorial, of honouring the dead, of our desire to create something lasting when a loved one dies.

Our little group carries on uphill after Stephen's Grave to White Tor, which has a large plateau surrounded by the remains of Bronze Age walls, huts and cairns. We roam among the strewn rocks but it is hard to make sense of them. We descend the other side, passing a funny little building built into the rock, presumably by the army for storing equipment. We pass a kist and then head towards a large standing stone. The map shows a double stone row leading off it but the stones are barely visible. From there, we strike out towards the stone circle, which is in a truly beautiful position, with Great Mis Tor rising up behind it, a dark, pointed triangle. Eventually we get there, but what a ruin it is: nothing like the 1894 picture. Only three stones are left standing. Apparently, it was vandalised by troops practising here in the Second World War. It looks sad and wounded. I feel angry at the destruction.

And yet this quest to find this stone circle is calming; it feels right. I feel this place chimes with my love for my dead son. Although it is ruined, its remains are a testament to something greater – to generations past, to people lost, to love itself. It feels like a receptacle of memory. A sanctum. The stones are a monument to the dead, like Felix's headstone, twenty miles away, bearing his name and his dates, another rock placed in the ground to remember someone.

Every day, most of every day in fact, I think about death and mortality. This is the consequence of Felix dying. These stones somehow embody that presence of death. These Bronze Age monuments are companions in my strange new life, somehow expressing and containing the loss and grief. They reflect the reality of what I am feeling. Their solidity is comforting. They trace our shared ancestry and history. They are about the dead, and the dead are always with us. They connect me to Felix.

15 July

Darling sweetie, it's been three months since I wrote to you, probably the longest gap ever. I just haven't been able to go there, to even think about the pain and sadness of your loss; I've just been plodding along, trying to survive. On the one hand, your death feels in the past, yet you are present everywhere, all the time. You are always in my thoughts and yet at the same time I rarely talk about you. The pain is just constant and I haven't been able to contemplate writing to you. I've been retreating, trying to hide from it all, but of course that doesn't work.

Yesterday was Dad's birthday. We had a party the night before, which was a great success but I really felt your absence – I could almost see it. We went to visit you at the Green Hill, which was beautiful. It is hot and dry at the moment, and the alliums on your grave are now beautiful big, round skeletal seed heads. We lay down for a while beside you. I brought you some sweet peas that a friend had given me.

I miss you so much, my darling Felix. I constantly wonder what you would be doing now. Giovanna went up to Edinburgh for her son Giac's graduation, and of course you, too, would have been graduating this summer. It's not just you I have lost, but your future. I have lost many other things. Part of myself. Part of my motherhood. My life as it was before. I am not the same.

I am trying to keep going, to keep doing the things I know keep me sane. One day, towards the end of the afternoon, I decide to head to Bell Pool, another of my haunts on the River Dart. I want to get out of the house, but I also want a bit of a longer walk — just to get away, be with my thoughts, be with Felix. As I arrive in the car park, the sun comes out. Tarka and I start walking through the woods amid a powerful, gleaming greenness, a kind of glow emanating from the trees. The leaves and bracken are bright, all dancing with sunlight, the surfaces wet from all the rain. We pass a large glade with the remains of a camp fire and reach the part of the track where, for some reason, Felix always played 'trains'. I remember this so clearly and always think about it at this stage of the walk. He would march along, his arms pumping back and forward like pistons, chanting 'chuff, chuff, chuff'.

I carry on beside the river. It churns and spurts over boulders, full from all the rain. We approach a little grassy clearing where I normally see pearl-bordered fritillary butterflies at this time of year. And yes, here they are! But they are hard to see because the bracken is so high this summer; the butterflies are flitting around the tops of the bracken, above my line of vision. Normally I can look down on them, admiring their complex markings and the chains of white pearls along the borders of their wings as they settle on top of the bracken, which is normally around the height of my chest. Today, I have to be content with viewing them from underneath. Still, it cheers me to see them.

On we go, climbing the path uphill away from the river, along craggy rocks, with scores of spindly oak trees bending down towards the Dart. Then it is a slither and a scramble back down to the river, with a bit of boulder-hopping before we finally make it to Bell Pool.

Oh, but it is beautiful: fuller than usual, brown but fairly clear water, with a canopy of acid-green leaves overhead. There is an island opposite, where local teenagers like to camp, and the pool is bordered by an enormous rock platform which you have to climb down an old iron ladder to get to. I enter the water with Tarka and the current is quite strong. I swim over to the other side and climb out over a very dark, almost black, burly-looking lump of rock. Tarka and I have a little explore of the island, finding the remains of a fire and a ragged piece of bunting. Then we get back in the river and I swim up to the waterfall, placing my face in the soft, foaming bubbles. I hover there, bracing myself on a rock, and keep my face immersed, watching the millions of spheres of light boiling under the water's surface. Then I let go and am swept downstream.

We used to come here a lot with the boys. I remember

when we first discovered the pool. We were walking along beside the river when the path started to rise perilously, winding up a cliff that seemed to appear out of nowhere. We were quite tired at this point in our walk, and nearly didn't bother to go any further. But we climbed that perilous path, and were so glad we did, because at the top we found ourselves looking down on an enormous pool with a waterfall, and a massive, almost rectangular bank of rock below us. We were surprised to see an old iron ladder screwed into the rock, leading vertically down from the top of the cliff. We wondered why it was there. Then we realised: this would be the perfect pool for catching sea trout. That's why the ladder was there. So, we climbed down it and sat on the rock in the sun, before taking turns to leap into the water, making enormous splashes as we did so. We returned there many times, spending afternoons lying on the rock and swimming.

12 August

Well, here we are again in Cornwall. Our third year here without you. And, of course, Grandpa is absent too. But we don't miss him in the same way we miss you. He was ninety-three. It was time for him to die. But you were taken from us cruelly, way too early, scandalously early.

Last night we sat around the dinner table, our depleted party —Kate, Ned, Tess, Ruby, Cosy, Matthew, James and Alex and Lucian — laughing and joking, and I felt so grateful for my family and the continuity and solidarity we have, of which you were part. And grateful that we get on (mostly) and have each other's support.

And later in bed, I thought back to the start of our extended family holidays together, over twenty years ago, when you were just a little baby; how they continued every year — you were a toddler, then a child, then a teenager, all of those happy times. You were an integral part of our family for twenty years and now you're gone. I think of us all crowded round the dinner table at Daymer Bay, our first holiday location, with Grandma and Grandpa at each end of the table, the rest of us squashed in on benches and mismatched chairs. I just felt so sad, so very sad, and tears started to form in my eyes as I lay there in the dark.

My brother Matthew has a plan to go and watch nightjars. They can, apparently, be seen on heathland on the Lizard. He has already visited and scouted out what he thinks will be the best spot, a place with various thickets where the birds like to lurk during the day, before coming out at dusk.

Matthew, Alex, Tess and I set off on a warm evening before sunset. There is golden light melting over the purple heather as we walk through the heathland. We sit down at the spot Matthew has found, and wait in silence. Slowly the light starts to dim. There is a short spell of pinkness over everything and then the colour fades to monochrome. I try not to feel bored, and to enjoy the sensation of seeing and feeling night fall. But I am not good at being silent and patient. I persist nonetheless. Tess plaits some grass. Tarka is slightly restless but starts to relax as we gradually change gear, moving into a period of quiet waiting. I start to enjoy the peace, the absence of noise and people, the growing darkness and the sense of anticipation.

We sit there for about an hour. Nothing happens. And

then, suddenly, there is a dark movement, like a phantom, from a nearby bush. It's a nightjar. It flies out of the thicket and disappears. It's just a glimpse, a magical glimpse, of this mysterious bird, like a ghost, a witness from another world.

Our mettle is up: we are alert, waiting for more nightjars. But there are none. That one dark form is all we see tonight.

On the last night of the holiday, we sit outside after dinner, marvelling at the night sky. It is absolutely littered with stars. The Milky Way is smeared across the heavens and the Perseid meteor shower is going off left right and centre. We sit there, faces turned upwards, watching for the meteors to appear. Suddenly, spark ! A squirt of light goes off in the night sky. And then, spark! Another! And another! This is the first time I've seen shooting stars and they keep surprising me. Spark! Spark! Small squirts of light are going off everywhere. The night feels enchanted.

We decide to go for a swim. As we enter the water, we are amazed to see our bodies surrounded by great swathes of twinkly-white diamonds. We all exclaim with delight. There are cries of 'Wow! Wow! This is sooooooo beautiful!' Lucian starts to kick his legs, and he looks as though he's propelled by some sort of underwater jet pack. We all try bigger manoeuvres and watch the trails of shimmering, sparkly delight run off our hands and feet: microscopic animals in the water emitting light. We all feel slightly hysterical and carried away.

Then we notice a huge orange thing on the horizon: we can hardly believe it's the moon. It was in a different place a few days ago. It is ludicrously, unrealistically orange.

Slowly it rises, an orange ball, becoming gradually whiter, casting a river of light on the sea.

We quieten down, taking in the dark sky, the shooting stars, the Milky Way, the bioluminescence. It's a magical conjunction where, somehow, we feel an unspoken connection to Felix.

We are there in the darkness, stars above us, stars below us, in a world that feels like heaven.

The suitcase

15 September

This doesn't get any easier; it really doesn't. I am randomly getting terrible feelings of utter pain and despair. I was just watching TV the other night and I suddenly found myself saying to Dad, 'Why did Felix have to die?' And was in floods of tears.

Clean Bandit's 'Rather Be', featuring Jess Glynne, has just come on the radio and it reminds me so much of you. You loved her voice. It is painful to hear.

Lucian is off to university in Sheffield next weekend. It naturally brings back thoughts of you at Leicester. And what you would be doing now, having graduated.

You were always such a great reader, as am I. But reading novels has become difficult. I just can't get interested, which used not to be the case. This is another way your death has changed me: lack of interest in things; not engaging with stuff in the out-side world. There's loads of Extinction Rebellion action at the moment and yet I just don't care about the impending end of the world. I don't have the emotional or intellectual space in my head. It's a shame I don't care, but there it is.

Your death has taken over my life in every way – my mind, my heart, my soul, my intellect, even my physical being.

My darling Felix, always loved.

It's there, in the top of the cupboard, the suitcase that I filled with Felix's special things after he died. It's been sitting there quietly, all this time. I know it's there but I haven't dared open it. I've wanted to but that desire has been outweighed by worry about the effect that opening it might have, of looking at and touching his things again. Will that set me off tumbling down another road of trauma and destabilisation? It's that dilemma I'm getting used to, of wanting to engage with his death but also pulling away. Trying to survive.

The suitcase is navy-blue plastic. I bought it for a few pounds in a charity shop in Torquay. It's not that big. It has silver clasps and is lined with striped pink-and-blue silky material. It's probably from the 1960s or '70s. It smells of old powder puffs. I remember my grandmother smelt like that. I bought it for putting Felix's things in. I wanted something old, second-hand, to be a special receptacle where his things could be safe until I felt ready to look at them. And then pack them away again.

Why are objects so important? They are aide-memoires. People may say they are only material things, but material things are bridges between ourselves and our feelings; they are signposts, they are symbols. These things are important. The material world is what we are. We are matter. We are things. We matter.

I open the cupboard door. There is the suitcase on the top shelf. I stretch up and reach for the handle, and feel the weight of the case push down on me. I place it on the bed. The top is dusty, with a nick out of it. Slowly I put my thumbs on the silver clasps. Flick. The clasps lift up. I grasp them and open the lid.

The first thing I see is paper. Handwriting. Folds in paper. Exercise books. The brim of one of his baseball caps sticking out from under something else. Some mouldy leather. Some official headed paper. Devon County Council. Devon Partnership Trust. The personal, the public, the private, the communication, both official and unofficial, that entered into and out of Felix's life.

I lift the top wodge of papers out. There's a card with a red kite on it, with a simple message from our friends Judy and Hilary after Felix died: 'You are in our thoughts.' Another one with a polar bear on, from another friend, Iona: 'This is just a little something to let you know I am thinking of you and hoping you have managed a few swims or dips. Sending much love.' Ah yes, I remember she sent me a beautiful swimming cap.

Next, a plastic folder containing official bumph. A letter from Leicester General Hospital about an appointment at the epilepsy clinic on Friday 16 June 2017 – well, he never made that. A bank statement he'd printed out for some reason, with payments to East Midlands Trains, iTunes, Domino's, Asda, Steamgames. His new concessionary Devon bus pass for the year, which arrived after he died and which I simply could not bear to throw away (he qualified because of his epilepsy). A partially filled-in application form to Leicester City Council for a disabled person's travel concession.

There's a loose piece of lined paper torn out from a notebook. It's notes on the 'French New Wave (1950s/early 1960s)'. I wonder if these notes were taken during a lecture? They are quite neat. Felix's handwriting is quite small and slopes to the right, with long, curled loops on the y's and g's. I read: '. . . *Era characterised by youthful spirit and desire for modernity . . . aim to rival Hollywood by creating quality over quantity . . . influenced by Italian neorealism . . . Breathless, 1960 Jean-Luc Goddard.*'

I realise I really knew nothing about what he felt about his studies – whether he enjoyed them, found them interesting, dull or challenging. I think I assumed he wasn't really taking them seriously, based on how he'd been in the sixth form, when he didn't seem inspired or motivated by learning. I realise we never talked about what he was up to in his degree. But then he hadn't been on the course for very long, and was more keen to talk about the plays he was in. But here, well, he was embracing a new intellectual world. There are more notes, on the history of film and of art. Then I come across something different.

Play – Modus Operandi (title for now).
Cast:
Maxine: Main female protagonist. Seen as the best doctor in her chosen area. (Brain surgeon?) Very high opinion of herself.
Joe: close friend. Job outside hospital. Friend from secondary school. Keeps Max's head on the ground (is that a

*phrase?). Always looking out for Max. Either female or
male, undecided.*
*Peter: receptionist. Cocky and bored of his job. Wanted to
be a surgeon but this is the best he can do. (blames Max?)*
*Sophie: Maxine's assistant – constantly striving for perfec-
tion (OCD?)*
*Phoebe: journalist who introduces Max to that which causes
her downfall.*

The paper crackles and smells musty. I pick it up and
sniff it, and try to think of Felix at his desk, writing in this
notebook. How come there are pages ripped out? He had
ideas. He was actively working on them.

Next, I find an acetate folder containing a laminated card
with Felix's picture on it. It is a head-and-shoulders shot of
him in school uniform, smiling, his dimples showing. Oh,
but he's beautiful. It is an International Baccalaureate student seating card for the IB exams he took in May 2015,
equivalent to A-levels and taken in six subjects across a
broad range of academic disciplines. With the card are several IB certificates showing his grades in his subjects of
English literature, philosophy, physics, Spanish, economics
and maths.

All these items and objects from his life, conserved in this
small blue suitcase. I dig around at the bottom. Here is his
wallet, a beautiful, buttery-soft leather wallet that Sean gave
him. It is covered in dusty grey mould. It's still got his school
bus pass in it from 2015. There's also a receipt from Spec-
savers from 2014. A receipt from McDonald's. A University of
Leicester Bookshop loyalty card. There's even a University
of Leicester Quidditch Society Membership card, 2015–16.
I hold the wallet. This was in Felix's possession, in his pocket,

next to his body. And what is it now? A relic, a mouldy relic, but it is precious all the same. It's something I can touch that he touched, that he possessed. There is a large jewellery box with his glasses and watch in it. His phone, too — dead, of course.

I am glad I have these things. They contain a fraction of his material essence, a physical remainder of his life. I can open this suitcase and look at and handle these things. These things that he carried; he touched. These things he wrote. These things to which he related, and which were a part of him. They are very precious. I don't feel devastated by encountering these objects. They are all I have left of him, in a material sense at least.

13 October

My darling, I have been thinking about Grandpa, and what a great age he reached. And I've suddenly realised how, all our lives, growing up, me and my brothers always knew about his brother Barry, even though, of course, we never met him. Barry was just there, part of the family. His framed picture was on the piano, alongside one of his Belgian girlfriend, Huguette. As you know, Barry was killed in the last months of the war, in 1945, when he was just twenty-three. Dad was only twenty at the time. Barry was a Royal Marine and was the first British soldier over the Rhine. This fact is marked on his grave in a war cemetery near Hanover.

I want to share some extracts from a couple of his last letters with you. I remember, growing up, the letters were kept in a tea caddy in the sitting room, and Grandpa would often look at them and show them to us. The first was written to Grandpa a few weeks before Barry died, in April 1945.

'We are in for another scrap soon, I shouldn't wonder. And I think that will be about the end. I have been wandering around Germany this afternoon and as far as I can see it will be no trouble at all. The countryside is loaded with the loot of Europe . . . There are several slave workers to every farm. The towns are absolutely flat. I have never seen anything like the devastation.

Must close now.'

The other letter was written the day before he died, to his father, your great-grandfather Walter. After giving news of the action, he says:

We have had no sleep now except for the odd nap for nearly 56 hours. Personally, I feel I do not need it. That is why I am writing now. I shall never catch it up if I don't start soon . . . Relief should be soon. I hope so . . . I am getting out of this commando. It is not what it used to be . . .

I am getting out because

a. I am getting a bit shaky though a rest might help.
b. I can't get on with the C.O. and shall get flung out sooner or later for F.A. as John Davis did.
c. I am stale in the job. I shall have held it a year in a month's time, most of it on active service which is a damn sight too long.

Altogether I think pastures new. We must close now. We shall probably be off again soon. However don't worry at this account of our doings. Casualties have been very small. Most of the time we fire and Jerry gives up.

All the best to all.

Love from BARRY

The suitcase

Oh, the cruel poignancy of that letter. Barry is wanting to get out. He is exhausted, and, in his words, 'shaky'. The next day he was killed. What must that letter have done to the family? It probably arrived after they got news of his death; what a heartbreaking thing that must have been to receive.

Dad never really spoke of the effect Barry's death had on him, although he spoke about Barry often and showed us his letters. We all understood how precious they were. However, he did say it haunted his father, your grandfather Walter, who visited the battlefield where Barry died several times, trying to understand what had happened. Walter was apparently tormented by questions about how Barry's death might have been avoided, so much so that it distressed the rest of the family a great deal, as he just wouldn't let it go. But this is so understandable when you learn that his own brother Stanley had been killed in the trenches in 1916, also aged just twenty-three, where they served in the same detachment.

At the time, the Bucks Herald *reported that Stanley, after presumably yet another squalid night in the trench, had, at 5:45 on a Saturday morning, 'being tired of doing nothing', got up to throw a bomb. He was immediately picked out by a German sniper who shot him through the head, killing him instantly. Walter was nearby when it happened. It quoted from a letter of condolence from the chaplain of the regiment, who said: 'It is my very sad duty as Chaplain to inform you that your son Private Stanley Pierce, of the 21ˢᵗ Royal Fusiliers, has nobly laid down his life in the cause of freedom and the defence of all whom he loved.' The newspaper went on: 'It was a pathetic coincidence that a quarter of an hour later than the time of his death, Private Pierce had hoped to leave the trenches, and that day he would have received a commission.' This last has uncanny echoes forward to Barry's death, in the fading months of the Second World War.*

Your death, at twenty, is equally senseless.

No wonder Grandpa was so utterly distraught when he heard the news. It was like history repeating itself. But I can learn from that; I can learn from my father's response to his brother's death, and how he carried him with him always. I can say your name, I can talk about you, I can take you forward with me, as a precious member of our family. It is perhaps more challenging than in the cases of Barry and Stanley. They gave their lives for their country. They were heroes. Not to have spoken of them would have been a betrayal of their sacrifice. You could argue their deaths served some sort of higher purpose: defeating the enemy. What purpose does your death serve? Nothing. Back then, death was common-place, young people were dying all the time. Now, it's a rarity, and talking about it is taboo.

When I bring you up in conversation, I often feel anxious about doing so. It's three and a half years since you died and I feel worried that people will think I'm shoving my misery down their throats, requiring or even demanding some sort of sympathy — that I am attention-seeking — and that your death is now well in the past. But I just want an honest conversation. I want to talk about you, my child, in the same way that any parent does, without even bothering to think about it.

I want to gather sloes and Rachel has told me there are some near Bench Tor. Tarka and I get out of the car and are buffeted by fearsome winds. We are right on the top of the moor, with nothing to protect us. The Dart rages in the gorge below. It is very squelchy underfoot as we cross a flat area and find a drystone wall where three small blackthorn bushes are braving the squall. I stand in the gale and pick. It is awkward and uncomfortable. I stand firm, bracing myself against the wind, and pick off the berries, contorting to pull down the branches to get the best fruits, all the while pricking my fingers and trying not to pick leaves and stalks.

I look up and notice some flocks of birds, swooping and turning together in one great movement, with white undersides and flashes of brown. There are large numbers of them wheeling in the wind. Occasionally, groups settle in the trees, only to curve off again into the air in a unified movement. What are they? I pull my phone out of my pocket and do a quick google. After a bit of scrolling, my best guess is that they are fieldfares — winter thrushes — who arrive here at this time of year. The birds continue to swoop and swirl. They are mesmerising in their unified, elegant movement. I stand in the wind, shivering and watching the visitors from faraway climes. I think about how they appear, and then disappear; ghosts from another world, they come and go.

I follow the wall, which turns a corner and heads downhill. I find more sloes, loads and loads, and carry on picking. This takes a while and Tarka gets bored and whiny. Eventually I'm satisfied, with two full carrier-bags, and we continue our walk down along the old pipeline from Venford Reservoir, which follows a contour through the woods above the Dart. The autumn colours are bright: browns, oranges, coppers, yellows and reds. I leave the main path by a fallen tree and follow a little track which emerges at Broada Stones, the central and remotest part of the Dart Gorge. It's somewhere I usually visit from the opposite bank, walking down from Dartmeet, and a place I have spent sunny afternoons with Felix, Alex and Lucian, as well as other family and friends.

Although the weather is foul, at least the wind finds it harder to penetrate into the depths of the valley. The river is running fast, with swirls of white foam, but there is a quiet eddy at the side. I strip off and immerse myself, floating with my eyes shut in this little backwater of calm as the Dart roars by. The water grips me in its coldness. No one knows where I am. Maybe Felix does? Is he here with me, in this water, in the fieldfares swooping above, in the sloes clinging to their spiny trees?

It is mid-November now and the weather all weekend has been vile, with endless rain and strong winds. Alex wants to go and photograph the Sherberton stone circle and we've been waiting for a weather window, but there is no sign of one. So, we set off at lunchtime, clad in waterproofs, hoping the weather will, as forecast, brighten up. As we drive, it starts to rain like stair rods, hammering on the car roof. We make the customary 'Oh, it's definitely brightening up over there' joke.

As we get out of the car we are assailed by gales and rain blowing straight at us. We cross the cattle bridge and set off down the lane towards the River Swincombe, commenting again, 'It's definitely brightening up.' It isn't. We cross the footbridge and the little river is more swollen than I've ever seen it. We talk about Felix, remembering walks here, and how good he was at map-reading.

I remember one particular occasion when I was here with Benj and Neal and the boys, taking them to see the stone circle. Without Alex navigating as usual, we got lost. Felix was the one who got out the map and worked out where we needed to go. I remember I was so proud of him for doing that. Another thing he was really good at was remembering number combinations for padlocks and key safes.

We reach the stone circle. It really has to be the least impressive on Dartmoor. It is even less impressive than I remember it from my previous visit. You can just about make out it was once a circle, but only a few of the stones remain in their original positions. Many have been moved and used to build a wall that cuts into the side of the circle.

There is an echo of memory that sounds when I go to a place Felix has been. Memory needs prompts, and places are good prompts. I love to hear that echo, even if it gets fainter over the years; an echo that says this person was here, their feet touched this ground, they breathed this air. Just like the people who made the stone circle thousands of years before.

21 November

My darling Felix, I haven't been to see you for about a month. It's dreary and dark, and I just somehow haven't managed to drag myself out of the house and into the cold and wet to see you. I am sorry. I want to come and see you, of course I do, but sometimes I shrink from it. It never gets any easier seeing your name and your dates — your mere twenty years — carved into that slate, the short facts of your existence. And yet I am thankful that you have some-where beautiful to rest, except of course you're not 'resting', you're dead, and if you're anywhere any more you're probably not there, in that field, where your flesh and bones are disintegrating.

Alex and I have to do a trip to the dump in Ivybridge so I have a quick look at the Ordnance Survey map to find a walk nearby. I notice a place called Burford Down, on Dartmoor, north of Harford, which has what looks like a very long stone row.

We park by the little and ancient Harford Bridge and enter the woods that border the River Erme. The ground is completely saturated. There are great pools of water full of autumnal leaves, in their oranges, yellows and browns. The river is running fast, bubbling and gurgling, rushing over boulders and cascades, keeping us company, chattering away. We notice the extensive remains of an unusual building on the bank. It is like a miniature aqueduct, with what looks like the remains of a wheel – an old hydroelectric plant, perhaps?

The path starts to ascend away from the river, and we climb, negotiating masses of moss-covered boulders of all shapes and sizes, which are scattered everywhere. They are very pretty but also fairly lethal, especially when combined with ankle-catching brambles. Finally, very hot and sweaty, we reach the top and the open moor, which is shrouded in mizzle as far as the eye can see. I stop to get my breath and admire the stark outline of a leafless little hawthorn tree, its branches edged with raindrops.

As we walk through the mist, we start to see a small tor ahead. This is Tristis Rock. It looks like a fortress or a castle keep, being a rather square shape. It is festooned with ivy and other vegetation, and a holly tree is growing out of the top. As we approach, we can see a dark hollow halfway up, almost like a window. It is somehow charming, this tor; it feels domestic, or like a turret in a fairy tale.

We clamber up the sides and stand on the flat top. Then

we descend and walk around it, looking closely at the riven granite. One side is covered with a vibrant patch of bright-green mosses, sedums and lichens, massed together. One of the mosses is a neon lime colour, an injection of light in the gloom. This small world of plant life living in the granite is uplifting on this grey day.

Very near Tristis Rock we find a cairn and a kist, marked on the OS map. They are very overgrown and there's not much to see; only part of the kist is visible. From there we walk to a cairn circle. Many of the stones are overgrown but the circle is quite distinct in the ground, and there is a small, bare hawthorn tree growing in the middle.

From the circle, a stone row heads off downhill into the distance. The stones are pretty small and, according to the map, stretch for about 400 metres directly north. Alex wants to follow them to the end but I am getting tired. He heads off, a black figure following the line of stones, disappearing into the mist.

I wait in the cairn circle, wondering who is buried here. There are potentially the remains of a number of people within the cairn circle and inside the nearby kist. Is the stone row an arrangement of gravestones? As I stand on my own, I think about my life and find it to be quite absurd. Here I am, wandering around in the mist on a dark November day, spending time among old rocks which, thousands of years ago, were placed in these positions by our ancestors. I'm on a desperate search for meaning. But it won't bring Felix back.

2 January 2020

Oh my darling, a new year begins.

Another year without you.

*There is a permanent ache in my heart. On Christmas Day —
our third without you — we went to the Green Hill. We opened
a present to you from Kate, a tiny jade F which we left hanging
on your tree. We gave you a tangerine and we lit a large, fat
candle that we left burning in a lantern for you. As we left the
graveyard, Lucian put his arm around me and I started to sob —
deep, heaving sobs. I needed to sob.*

*Yaara had a party on New Year's Eve, which I wasn't in the
mood for at all. At 7.45 I was still lying on the bed, not dressed,
not ready or willing to go out, but I forced myself. It was actually
lovely — an Indian meal followed by a silly game — but I left
before midnight as I didn't want to sing 'Auld Lang Syne'.*

*Then the following day we went to Hope Cove as usual: our
annual New Year's Day swim in a place called Hope. It was our
tenth year. It was a dull day but it was a flat sea, and it was
Catherine's fiftieth birthday. We sang 'Auld Lang Syne' in the
water and I was OK with that. Then we went out for Catherine's birthday lunch. We sat, dear friends and their children,
and, of course, Lucian, and I felt your absence so strongly, so
desperately strongly. We filled the table and it felt as though there
should have been an extra space for you. I don't know what I feel
about the forthcoming year. I don't really feel anything.*

In the middle of February, I head to Malta with Milla, her
daughter Nelia, who is my god-daughter, and Nelia's
friend Emily. There have been international murmurings
about a deadly virus that has taken hold in China, but we

are fine, it seems, to travel. It doesn't seem to be affecting us here in the West. It is to be a girls' week in the sun. We have a vast apartment in an enormous block in Sliema, with fantastic views out to sea and over to the ancient walled town of Valletta. Malta is a bit odd, with its signs in English everywhere, but it is the perfect place to be at this time of year when it's so grey in England. It is bright and warm, and, even better, everywhere we go there seem to be convenient rocks for us to swim off, many of them with little steps, ladders and handrails in various states of disrepair. The sea is shimmering and turquoise.

One day, Milla and I get the ferry over to Valletta and wander around. It is rather charming, feeling as though it is stuck in the 1960s. We pass a record shop with a 'His Master's Voice' sign over the door, and another one selling 'holy communion and confirmation suits made to measure'. There is a haberdasher with scores of lace trimmings on display. We visit St Paul's Shipwreck Church, a camp vision where the walls are lined with shocking-pink taffeta. Then we wander around the northern end of town and find a lovely swimming spot, with a rock-cut pool and views out into the Mediterranean. An old man is fishing off a rocky outcrop, with several cats hanging around him. The water is clear and fresh, and we lie on the rocks to dry off. And then the most enormous ship hoves into view. It is the ferry from Sicily, dwarfing everything around it.

Felix's birthday falls while we are there. I haven't prepared for it; I just couldn't face thinking about it. I decide to get a photo of him on my phone printed out. I find a print shop, which does the job, and then choose a frame. The shopkeeper doesn't charge me for the frame. Does he somehow know? Then we try to find a cake. It seems cakes aren't really the thing in Malta, so we settle for a Viennetta ice cream we find in the supermarket. Felix was actually a real fan of Viennetta so it feels quite appropriate. After dinner, I put out his photo, place candles on the ice cream and we raise our glasses to him. I feel emotional, but it's OK. I'm not distraught. Like last year, I am away from home, and I feel that helps.

Year Four

The virus

22 March 2020 – Mother's Day

Oh my darling. This is such a strange day. Amid strange, strange times. Mother's Day is always so mixed for me. Joy that I am mother to two amazing young men. Terrible sadness that you are not here. I still can't believe you're not here. I love you.

And now the country is in the grip of a plague. The Corona-virus. It feels biblical, apocalyptic. From tomorrow we will be confined to barracks in unprecedented times. Pubs, restaurants, cinemas will be closed. No socialising. Life will go on pause.

When it first started, my thoughts immediately turned to you. How would it have affected you? This is another major thing you are not part of, not experiencing. Eventually it will pass. But not for some time, I suspect.

For the moment, life is on hold. We have to appreciate the small things, the little things, find beauty in them, solace in them, even.

I visited your grave a few days ago. The clump of primroses we planted when you first died is flourishing, floribundant, looking gorgeous. Also, Rachel gave me a hellebore, which I planted, which is looking good, and a few weeks ago I put in some cowslips, which appear to be flowering, though somewhat early.

Normal life has ended abruptly. A couple of days ago, the lockdown came into force. Before that, when it became apparent it was imminent, we had to rush up to Sheffield to get Lucian and bring him home before everything shut down. So now, there are three of us in the house, in our so-called 'bubble'.

Suddenly, there are no cars on the roads. We can't go anywhere unless on foot. I take Tarka out for our usual walk up the Terrace, a large field on a hill opposite our house. As I set off down the street, I see another person approaching. As he gets nearer, he crosses the road. Is that because of the new 'social distancing', I wonder?

Tarka and I turn off the road and climb up the granite staircase that leads to the Terrace which is overhung with elder. At the top, I put my hand out to open the gate, but then stop. Maybe I'd better not touch it with my bare hand? I slide my hand up my sleeve and use the sleeve as a glove. We set off up the muddy track, passing our old house down below. I see the window of Felix's bedroom and think back to the time we discovered him unconscious, having a seizure for the first time. I think of all that happened there, up to and including Felix's death. And now, to current events, to a bigger sense of loss bearing down on us all, with a virus that is cruising around the world, leaving death in its wake.

To a certain extent I feel a sense of relief. There is a bitter, smug part of me that is glad everyone else is catching up with what we, as a family, have already experienced. Of course, no one can know or understand that specific loss of Felix, but perhaps they are feeling that sense of a world shattered, torn apart, fundamentally changed in an utterly alien way. A feeling of suddenly finding yourself wandering around in a world that feels unfamiliar and strange. The pandemic has thrown our accepted normality upside down. Suddenly, we have lost our freedoms and our certainties. To me, it just feels so familiar.

Maybe there's an upside. I can completely retreat from the world. I no longer have to participate. I can curl up inside and keep the world out. I will no longer have to go out to events or to negotiate situations. I need no longer pretend or dissemble.

13 April

This is such a strange time my darling. We are confined to home and our immediate vicinity. I've been having to walk to my usual swim spots, which is certainly making me realise how lazy I am usually! The two nearest are each about forty-five minutes' walk, which does mean that what is normally a 'quick dip' now takes at least a couple of hours. But in this new world, does that really matter? Luckily the weather is so beautiful — it seems to be permanently sunny, so walking is a pleasure.

Yesterday I went to the Queen of the Dart. You remember it, that pool to the south of town, named after a copper mine that was there in Victorian times? I schlepped up the road towards the moor, then diverted down that old track opposite the tatty farm. The roads were wonderfully empty. It was so quiet and peaceful. As I walked down the final stretch, Summerhill Lane, I saw a host of spring flowers growing out of the high Devon banks: clouds of white stitchwort, violets like little purple jewels, blackthorn blossom and primroses. There were lots of shiny, green wild garlic leaves bursting through too. Then, alongside the river, there were great swathes of wild daffodils, and wood anemones – little white stars clustering under the trees.

Beside the river, as I stood on the sandy bank avoiding the large cowpats, contemplating the water, I thought about you. How, in this time where I've suddenly been freed from various constraints, I may now have more time for you. And yet, it doesn't really change anything. I suppose it has removed external pressures, which is a good thing. Anyway, I found great solace in wading slowly into the clear, clean river, launching my body into the cool, dark centre of the pool, and swimming over to the young beech tree that overhangs the other side. I lay on my back and looked up at the tree's branches spreading above me, about to come into leaf. I was alone, but I didn't feel alone; I felt you were there with me, somehow present.

We're getting used to being on our own at home. It is quite a novelty not using the car. One Sunday, Alex suggests walking from home to Rippon Tor, a distance of about four miles, pretty much all uphill. We usually drive to our moorland walks. It will be a bit of an adventure, and a day out.

We head out along the lane from our house, enjoying the warmth of the sun on our bodies. Alex has a large stick, which he swings as he walks, and Tarka jumps up at it, as though she's on springs, bouncing like a woolly ball. We trudge uphill, getting hotter all the time. Eventually we make it to the cattle grid, which marks the start of the moor, and the Dartmoor National Park 40mph sign saying *Take Moor Care*, which is pockmarked with bullet holes. I've always wondered who shot those holes in it, and why. By the cattle grid is a stand of pine trees, where we stop and rest on a log. We look up at the trees gently moving in the breeze, their dark-green, graceful tops meeting above our heads like stone tracery in a cathedral ceiling.

Then we're back on the road for a short way, before turning off onto the open moor, past the old army rifle range, an ugly, red-brick edifice that looms up out of nowhere like a 1970s prog-rock album cover. Then we pass a ruined Bronze Age settlement, in the lee of Rippon Tor. It has a large network of field boundaries, or reaves, as well as several hut circles. We pass a babbling stream, the sunlight glistening through the bubbles in the water, and the stones on the bed shining. We're getting ever higher, and then we're on the final ascent to Rippon Tor, with a commanding view down over Haytor. As we stand look-ing across the valley, and down to the sea at Teignmouth, we see police cars patrolling the road leading to Haytor, presumably sending lockdown-breaking motorists home.

At last, we reach the summit, 473 metres above sea level. In the old days it was apparently known as Raven Tor, with the surrounding area known as Raventor Common. There are three large cairns here, one built on top of the tor itself. Three grand burial places with views as far as the eye can see.

Standing at the top, we turn around slowly, admiring the tors that encircle us below, like citadels. To the east and north-east are Bag Tor and the twin peaks of Haytor. Ahead of us are Saddle Tor and Holwell Tor, and then, turning north-west, Greator Rocks, Hound Tor and Honeybag Tor. Turning to the west and south-west, we spy Top Tor, Pil Tor and then, to the south-west, Buckland Beacon. The latter is our local tor, visited so many times we have lost count – a place we've been on high days and holidays, on ordinary days, happy days and sad days. It's where Alex and Lucian went the day they learned Felix had died, when I was still in Leicester. They took a daffodil for him and left it on the rock.

17 May

Oh my darling. Four years on from your death and I'm hanging out your washing again. We had a clear-out and I found a drawer full of your clothes that I'd kept. I remember at the time I just couldn't reduce your clothes down to just a few items. So, now I'm washing them again: shirts, jeans, hoodies, pegging them out in the sun and wind, which makes me both happy and sad at the same time. I will give some of this final set of your clothes away but will keep some. In particular, your MED Theatre and Leicester University Theatre hoodies. I will keep them and wash them from time to time, my ritual of remembering, of keeping you present. I will also wear them.

Sometimes I feel that those months after you died, I was the most alive I have ever been: living your loss totally, experiencing that agony of grief, like being in love, almost – that ecstasy and intensity of feeling, not eating or sleeping.

The world I knew had been torn apart – wolves had come and attacked me in the night, and sunk their teeth into my flesh, and ripped me apart. They left me for dead on the forest floor, and I came round, bleeding and wounded.

I lived in a whirlwind of emotions. I couldn't do anything but feel, even though I was in a sort of dreamlike state at the time, which was also of course not a dream but a nightmare, a harsh, cruel reality of a nightmare. Part of me looks back to that time with a kind of fondness. No one expected anything of me; I was allowed to live my grief, to be mad, to be estranged from the world in my agony.

Now, in a way, I am healed, but I just feel numb and I want to numb myself with swimming, walking, alcohol, experiences, busyness.

The lockdown has finally ended. Today I had a humdrum task: to go to the supermarket in Newton Abbot. As I was driving in to this dreary town, I thought of all those years driving to swimming lessons on Monday night, the weekly tedium of getting you changed and into the pool, and sitting sweating while you had your lessons. The pain of your death blindsided me again as I sat in the car: the cruelty of your life cut short, your complete absence, the snuffing out of your life.

But then, later, the day got better. It became beautiful, sunny and warm. Rachel and I went down the Yellow Brick Road. The bluebells were spilling down the little valley to the river, a sheen of blue against the ramrod-straight electric-green shoots of bracken. We swam in Black Pool, the water high and foaming. I put my head properly under for the first time this year and the bubbles caressed my face, and I laid a boulder for you — a smooth, round, small one — and I loved you.

I wake early and feel restless. What shall I do? I don't feel like going back to sleep. Then I have an idea: watch the sunrise. It always makes me feel better. I check the phone and the weather is clear. Quickly, I dress, and Tarka and I head off to the moor. We cross the cattle grid with its habitual rumble and I drive along, unsure where to go. I have a tradition of watching from the old firing range, but I want to go somewhere different. Then it strikes me: Saddle Tor. It faces east.

We often used to go to Saddle Tor with the children. It's just by the more famous Haytor, beloved by thousands of Dartmoor tourists. It's a good climbing and sledging spot and is conveniently near the road for small legs (and lazy adult ones). Its twin grey granite outcrops are linked by a smooth, grassy plateau – the saddle.

It is already light, with a pinkness over in the east, as I start climbing the tor. There is a cold wind and, as I reach the top, the sun is not yet risen, though there is a glow forming where it should be. There's a few more minutes until sunrise so I walk down the other side of the tor, to kill some time, and then retrace my steps back to the top, to find somewhere to settle in and watch the spectacle.

I find a perfect niche in the northerly outcrop, sheltered from the wind. I sit, enclosed by three walls, looking out to the east. I focus on the point on the horizon that is lightest, by the Teign estuary and the sea beyond. Suddenly, I see a gleaming pink-orange dot in the distance. Gradually it expands, molten, and, before my eyes, the sun rises up, a burning ball of power and energy. It is magical, mysterious, reassuring and frightening all at the same time. It draws me like a moth to a flame. Why do I find it so compelling? It is like God, or an absence of God, or the presence of something, whatever that might be – something bigger than me, at any rate. It is always there, whether I am or not, rising and setting, every day, eternal. It is both of our world and apart.

Somehow, it reeks of time. It drips with time, and also with immortality; with our incapability of understanding or beating time. We, in our little, parcelled-up lives, try to challenge time. But nothing, and no one, can. Is Felix in that burning ball, rising and falling every day? I feel connected with him at these moments of transience, of liminality, when night is turning into day. The threshold moments of dawn and dusk feel like momentary portals into eternity, or, at least, into a world where life does not have physical form in the way that we know it.

Everything around me is bathed in gentle, pink light. The heather and bracken are glowing. I turn and look behind me, and as far as the eye can see there is pink light. I continue to watch the sun as it gets bigger and bigger, filling the sky until eventually it loses its form and is just light.

23 June

My darling, I am not writing so much to you these days. I don't feel the need. Part of me feels sad about this. But another accepts that the letters could never have continued in quite the same vein. The reality is that I no longer feel that desperate urge to write to you as I did when you first died. And yet I think of you every day; several times every day. Gradually, you are becoming part of me in a way you weren't before. I am no longer Sophie, going forward. I am Sophie and Felix going forward. You are absorbed into me, like a Siamese twin, grafted into my being: I carry you everywhere.

*Of course, I am still ransacked by moments of terrible grief.
But I am learning to live my life with you by my side emotionally, mentally, spiritually, if not in physical reality. You are there,
present, in my thoughts the whole time. Every experience is now
shaped by the fact that you are dead. I seek out those things
which bring me closer to you, in a metaphysical connection.*

I am down by the sea at Thurlestone. It is an overcast and
febrile day. There is blue sky in the distance, but over the
sea there are grey, oppressive clouds. The wind is strong.
White horses and kite surfers are scooting about on the
surface of the sea, being blown this way and that.

Alex is collecting seaweed.

It is low tide.

I am swimming among the rocks, where I am exploring a maze of channels and gullies. The water is grey and
murky and still. Beyond, out in the open water, the sea
surges and rages. I feel calm, engaged, moving past curtains of seaweed hanging at eye level, watching them
suddenly glisten, transformed, every time the sun comes
out. And then equally suddenly, they retreat back into
murk when the sun goes in again. It's as though someone
is turning the lights on and off. I swim through and alongside fat strips of purple dulse, rubbery wracks, bright-green
slimy weed. I see circles on the rocks, the homes of limpets, temporarily vacated while they are off hunting. I see
a snakelocks anemone exposed out of the water – fat,
shiny and greeny-grey with its purple tentacles tucked in.
I enjoy quietly swimming among the weed, feeling the
rocks and sand beneath me, meandering aimlessly, following the gullies into dead ends and out again. Eventually

I follow one channel towards the open sea, where there is moving water and swell. I let myself be sucked out, pulled and pushed by the waves. I am consumed by the sea, immersed in its shapelessness.

Afterwards, I sit among the rocks and remember a trip to this very beach when Felix's paternal grandparents, Lesley and Paul, were visiting. It was a very hot, sunny day. The boys wore their wetsuits and played in and around these rocks where I've been swimming today, except it was high tide. They jumped and dived off the rocks into the pools and gullies. They were here. Felix and Lucian were here. It seems so strange now. Are they somehow still here?

I remember another occasion, a very long time ago, when we visited another beach, just round the corner, when the boys were about ten and seven. It was an incredibly hot day, so hot we could hardly walk on the sand. That is the only time I've ever experienced sand as hot as that in Devon. It was roasting and we all spent a lot more time in the water than usual.

If Felix had lived, I probably wouldn't be dredging up memories like this as I sit on this beach. He would still be physically present in my life so I wouldn't need to do that. However, alone here today, I actively try to mine those happy times from the past. It is good to remember, almost to try to conjure up his presence.

In some way, am I closer to him now than if he had lived? Hardly – that's wishful thinking. But I feel he occupies a greater part of my mind and heart than he would have done if he were still alive. If he were still here, making his own way in the world, earning a living, having a family, he would not preoccupy me to the same degree or indeed in the same way.

Looking at my feet in the sand, I feel the grains between my toes and think of the millennia that this sand has existed in this world, in different forms perhaps – as rocks in different places, as shells, all being moved around by the sea and ground down into what it is today. Matter is neither created nor destroyed. So, are we all still somehow alive when we are dead, but in a different form? I think, somehow, we are – but not 'alive' as we know it. If we are ash and dirt, we are no longer sentient. But, somehow, we continue to exist.

Not far from here – about 10 miles – is the Green Hill. Beside it flows the Dart, which comes out into the sea at Dartmouth, just along the coast. Felix's remains in the earth on the Green Hill will, perhaps, travel down the river and out to sea, and eventually, perhaps, to this spot, in some form.

There are young families all over this beach reminding me of past times. The story didn't turn out as it was supposed to. All these families have expectations, as indeed did we. There is nothing wrong with expectations, except they should never be the focus. The focus should be the precious present, and yet here I am thinking about the past. Back then, I don't think we were really thinking much about the future. In fact, maybe we didn't really have expectations, as such. We just assumed life would turn out a certain way. But it didn't.

Hoar frost

3 December

My darling Felix, the second lockdown has ended and I am sit-
ting in one of the loveliest places in the world. I'm in a nook
among the rocks at Bugle Hole, above a turquoise diamond of sea
I've just swum in. Do you remember coming here at low tide
when we found the pink tunnel? You and Lucian climbed through
a hole in the rocks and disappeared. Then we heard your voices
far away, and it turned out the hole led to a passage that con-
nected to another beach on the other side. Inside, the rock was
pink and glistening; it was like being inside a giant's gullet. It
was slippery and echoey and grotesque, fairytale unreal.

Now, I like to come here at high water, to swim in the pool
that forms when the tide is in. Centuries ago, someone cut some

steps into the rock by where I am sitting — little steps to access the water. They were probably used by smugglers. Now, they are treacherous, covered in slippery green seaweed.

It is windy and the gulls are constantly crying overhead. When I was in the water, I closed my eyes and felt myself being pulled up and down by the swell. The water washed against my body and the breeze ruffled my face. I thought of you. Of times here past. Of many, many times when you and Lucian were small, on Mothecombe Beach just down the coast from where I am today. We always used to walk around from the main beach, over the rocks, to what we regarded as our 'secret' beach. I remember many rock-pooling expeditions. The best catch ever was of a pair of five-bearded rocklings, grotesque little brown fish with spooky spikes around their faces.

The rocks where I am sitting are full of purple stripes, with lots of little round holes. They feel volcanic. This is an enclosed, secret little place, with happy memories. And memories, to me now, are as real and valid and as alive as present, lived experiences. In the end, nothing really has any meaning, unless we give it meaning. I could be sitting here, blankly, thinking of nothing. But I give this place meaning — or at least, it has meaning for me. And that is something I can do: nurture my memories, foster them, maybe even embellish them. That is my truth. You are in those memories, Felix, you are part of my essence, my mind, my memory, my existence. You are in this water that rises and falls and ebbs and flows in this circle of rocks, twice a day, into eternity or whenever the world ends. You are in that water in the stream I see before me, rushing down over the rocks and into the sea pool below. I love you, Felix.

The love for a child is really about the love of oneself, about one's very existence. After all, why do we love our children? It is not because of any of their attributes. We love them because they

are ours, produced by us, produced by our physical bodies, and
because of something we did – they came from us. We love them
because they are life, existence itself. If we didn't love them, we
wouldn't be interested in loving, surviving, playing a part in this
life and this world. So, the death of a child is the death of part of
us. Your death, Felix, is the death of part of me.

I wake up and feel cold. Time to set off for the Sunday
swim, my regular fixture with friends in the Dart, which has
been so disrupted during the pandemic. I get my thermals
on and head out to the car, which is covered in thick swirls
of frost. I rummage around to find the scraper and work
away at the crust, feeling a sense of trepidation about swimming today; this is the first cold weather of the winter – it's
been warm and wet so far. I drive up the hill out of Ashburton and there is bright sun lighting up the higher ground. At
New Bridge there is ice in the car park. We set off along the
river to Spitchwick, the oak leaves underfoot stiff and edged
with frills of frost like candied fruits. We emerge onto the
common, which is white with frost. Everywhere is in tones
of grey and white. The cliff behind the river is a stern
expanse of cold rock and muted mosses.

We start to change and there is much speculation about
the water temperature. Judy, as usual, is first in. There is a
thick bed of leaves rotting on the river bed, only slightly
softening the blow of entering the water. I step in gingerly
and can feel little needles endlessly pricking my skin – pointy
daggers! The first instance this winter of this, one of our
numerous terms for the varying states of cold. As I plunge
in, I feel the river grab my shoulders and the back of my
neck in its cold clasp. *Brrrrrrrr!* It is *so* bracing! Judy declares

it is 3.1 degrees – about 3 or 4 degrees colder than when I was last in, a few days ago. I last about two minutes.

Afterwards I am thinking, *Why? Why do I go to the bother of leaving the house on a freezing-cold morning, willingly take my clothes off and plunge into icy-cold water?* It is quite simply the buzz. I feel alive, as though I have really engaged with life itself, been absorbed, been part of nature, got away from civilisation and worldly cares. I desperately feel the need to grab life with both hands, to live it viscerally. I know what it is to lose it.

Also, with this Sunday swim fixture, it is about being here every week. Seeing the river and my friends in all their seasons, colours and moods. It gives life richness, a seam of continuity through thick and thin. And it is a backdrop, a benchmark, against which life is measured, against which things happen, good and bad. This all started well before Felix died, and has continued since. And those friends have been a constant in my worst times.

Later, Alex and I head off to Princetown to find a Bronze Age village on the slopes of Hart Tor. We park on the road just south of Princetown and cross the tiny River Meavy. We make our way over a lumpy area of ground worked by tinners in the past, full of depressions and bumps. We follow a small path uphill towards Hart Tor and start to see the telltale rings of stones to our left. We break away from the path and find a huge array of hut circles of every size. The first we come across is small and almost perfectly formed, with walls two to three stones deep, with a distinct and clear shape.

Families lived here, 3,000 years ago, in these little thatched roundhouses. Families with children and aunts and uncles and cousins and mothers and fathers who loved each other and probably died before they were thirty.

Alex tells me that many of these ancient homes were excavated at the end of the nineteenth century; the remains of eighteen roundhouses were fully revealed, but there were many more than that, their traces visible in raised areas of ground. Some have extremely large double-height granite blocks as part of their walls, which I have never seen before. Perhaps they used a big rock that was already there as a starting point?

The day is sunny and clear. We walk on to Hart Tor, from where the views are awe-inspiring: down to the sea and Burrator Reservoir, the latter glinting in the light like a big mirror laid on its side. We descend from the tor down to Hart Tor Brook and find a massive boulder on the way, a huge round piece of rock, about twice my height, that looks as though it's just been plonked there on the moor, chucked down by some mythical being. It's called the Giant's Marble – a most appropriate name. I walk around the back of it and am astonished to see some rather outlandish-looking lichen. It's green with scarlet tips, clinging all over the back of the rock like a rash. I've never seen anything like it. Tiny and intriguing, it is a whole miniature world of life inhabiting the northern side of the rock (there's none on the sunny southern side). Later, I look it up and discover it's called red soldier lichen, or matchstick lichen.

From here we cross the brook and have a steep climb through muddy puddles. Halfway up the hill, we find what I call 'Dartmoor snot' – grey globules on the ground. It's a bizarre substance I have only ever seen here on Dartmoor. Apparently, its name is star jelly – some believe it is a deposit from falling meteors. Others believe it may be a slime mould, of which there are about 350 species in the UK. However, the latest theory is that it's the remains of the oviducts of frogs, which, from autumn, are full of spawn. The frogs have been eaten by birds, which may have spat out the oviducts as they don't taste nice. My favourite supposition comes from the *Legendary Dartmoor* website, whose author Tim Sandles says, 'Maybe the jelly on Dartmoor is "Piskie Puke" and is the result of a heavy night on too much Cowflop Juice at a Piskie Revel.'

We make it up to the plateau at the top to Cramber Tor, an unremarkable low collection of rocks except for a strangely geometric arrangement on top that makes a perfect place to sit and look at the views, which are even more spectacular than from the top of Hart Tor, which is 390 metres high; Cramber Tor is about 50 metres higher. We sit and look down at the world below us: Dartmoor, spread out in its bleakness and beauty; the sea, in the distance. A world where life continues, even though for us, life has in some way stopped.

After a little rest, we set off north-west from Cramber Tor. The ground is very boggy despite the fact we are on a plateau. We are thankful it is a clear day as the path is not distinct at all and it's the sort of place where you could get lost very quickly if the mist came down.

We come across a small pond, frozen over, with weeds at the edge trapped under the ice. In the summer it probably dries up. If it were deep enough to swim in, it would be like swimming on top of the world.

From here, it is another boggy tramp to South Hessary Tor, which is like a natural, rock climbing frame, with lots of ledges. People are sitting on top, admiring the views. Finally, we walk up Conchies Road to Princetown, where we tuck into a savoury cream tea with chips at the Fox Tor Cafe.

Hoar frost

15 December

Darling Felix, I am thinking about everything that has happened in the last few years. The deaths of my son, my mother and my father. I've had to become so tough. The enormity of what has happened to me is suddenly striking me again. And the eternal question, again: where are you?

Well, one thing I do know is you are inside me — inside my heart, inside my lungs, inside my stomach and liver and bile duct and pancreas and every other single part of me.

Mariah Carey has just come on the radio: 'All I Want for Christmas is You.'

Suddenly I'm wracked with sobs.

It is properly *wintry*. For a few days now we've had frosts, ice on the roads, and quiet stillness. Alex and I head up to the moor, surprised by how foggy it is up high; it was clear at home in Ashburton. We park at Cross Furzes, not far from Buckfast Abbey, and set off down the holloway that leads on to the open moor. Its high sides are lined with bright-green moss, even though it's the middle of winter. Ferns are growing out of the moss and altogether the walls look so alive, so verdant in the icy scene.

We cross the Dean Burn using the lovely low clapper bridge with its unusually long granite slabs. One is stamped 1972 and the other has a less clear date, possibly 1705.

Along this route, I always feel the ghosts of walkers before me: the monks who used this track to travel between the abbeys on Dartmoor, and before that the jobbers transporting wool. And in the second decade of the twenty-first century, Alex, Felix, Lucian and I.

We walk among gnarled beech trees, with their smooth, elephantine trunks, to emerge onto the slopes of Dartmoor through fields where cattle suddenly appear, dark bodies in the mist.

We start to notice the frost. It makes everything look like a fairy wonderland or over-the-top Christmas card. Every individual blade of grass is edged with white. Clumps of grasses we would never normally notice are glammed up as though for a night out, each blade sparkling with diamante. We pass a hawthorn tree that has great curtains of lichen hanging from its branches. At first, we think there are two sorts of lichen, but on closer examination we realise that each individual strand is encrusted with frost, crisp to the touch.

This is so unusual these days, with our warm, wet winters. How wonderful to be experiencing winter properly, with iron-hard ground, crisp, biting air, and shades of white and grey all around, trees, hedges and plants all metamorphosed into white creatures of winter.

And water like a stone.

As we get higher, we occasionally hear voices. But we can't see anybody. We walk alongside the vast Avon Dam Reservoir, knowing it's there but not able to see it. Of it there is no sound, no sound at all, and we feel strangely isolated, wrapped in mist and on our own little pathway. We're almost frozen in place and time.

We are hoping to find some hut circles and a settlement that we know are right next to the path. Thanks to our Ordnance Survey app, we can tell exactly where we are, despite only being able to see a few yards ahead. We manage to find several large hut circles, including one with two remaining door jambs. We then follow the boundary wall of the settlement back to the path before carrying on to where we think we can walk down to the top of the reservoir. We find our way down and are greeted by the gurgling sound of a stream that leads into the body of water. Although we know the lake is really near, we still can't see it. Eventually, we find ourselves right on the bank, where we see an expanse of ice, with a tufty little island. I had hoped to swim here but it feels way too cold and exposed, quite apart from the fact the water is frozen.

We return to the path. We stop to have our lunch near an icy ford, an area that, according to the map, must have been quite busy in the old days, as it is at a crossroads of tracks. There are actually three fords, and pillow mounds, created by warreners to keep their rabbits in. There are cairns, settlements and something called Huntingdon Cross, which is written on the map in Gothic script. We can't actually see any of these features as we sit in the fog on a random pile of stones eating our soup. But it's good to know they are there; to have a sense of this place's history and meaning – or, at least, meaning in the context of human experience.

We get up and continue our journey around the northern side of Hickaton Hill, through featureless, tufted landscape. We keep seeing rabbit droppings on the path. We come off the moor at Lud Gate and return along the lane where I remember, one autumn, we unexpectedly found a huge patch of chanterelles clinging to the moss-covered stone walls, an orange rash against the bright-green moss. The boys were with us and we ransacked our pockets for bags, filling them with the delicious mushrooms.

A storm

3 January 2021

Oh my darling, nearly four years on from your death, I feel you are now moving into a different realm. I think I am OK with that, though I am not sure. Before, I felt you sinking, disappearing, moving away from me like water through my fingers, or a lump of stone inevitably dropping into a dark abyss, never to be seen again. Now, though, I feel you are there, but in a different, separate place. I don't feel you're going to disappear or fade away any more. Is this acceptance? I don't know. I can never accept that you died. Except, maybe, I am starting to? I don't like the thought of that. And yet maybe that is a good thing? Because accepting that you died doesn't mean I don't love you any more or that you don't exist any more. You do exist – in my emotional

234

life, in my heart, you are there, you are not going anywhere. In your separate realm, wherever or whatever that is, you are always there, beside me, with me, part of me always.

A Facebook memory pops up from a decade ago, of a walk to a tiny river near South Brent called the Glaze Brook, leading to a waterfall with a plunge pool. This was when the boys were about fourteen and eleven. There was quite a gang of us: Neil and Clare, who was pregnant, Catherine and Alex with their children Joseph and Lizzie, along with Esther, Angie, Judy, Justine and Kari.

I remember that day very well. It was dry and sunny and cold as we walked out across the moor. We heard the river before we saw it – a rushing gurgle over rocks. When we found the waterfall, we were enchanted. It was in a tree-filled dell, and the photos show us larking around, swinging from a rope that dangled over the centre of the pool and sitting at the bottom of the waterfall, getting deluged. In his famous *Guide to Dartmoor*, William Crossing writes of this spot: 'Here are great boulders of granite, some with coats of moss, ferns and heather, and sturdy hawthorns, a charming cascade, and a dark pool over which trees spread their branches. This is the Wishing Pool, and it is said that those who leap across it, and while doing so loudly express a wish, will obtain what they desire.'

I look at the pictures again. It is actually a totally magical scene. I zoom in on one of the photos. I look at it, really look at it. It is just beautiful: the white waterfall in the centre, pouring down into an oval pool. Either side of the pool are rocks and trees, smothered in moss-like, luscious, green velvet. And below the trees, covering the banks, great piles of coppery leaves, some lit up by the sun's spotlight.

I'm in my wetsuit, swinging out across the water, with my mouth unflatteringly open, obviously hooting with laughter. And then I see Felix to the side, on the bank, watching. I zoom in more. There is his beautiful face, clad in his woolly hat with flaps over the ears, looking up at where the rope is straining on the branch from which it hangs. My darling, beautiful boy, with just the tiniest start of growth on his upper lip, his profile highlighted by the sun, preserved in a sunbeam, there by the little river. My heart hurts.

It's a boring Saturday, with constant drizzle. With nothing better to do, I decide, on the spur of the moment, to go back to the scene of that photo. I drive along the small, winding lane that leads to Owley Moor Gate. The road is potholed and flooded. I pass an ancient farm that straddles the road – barns on the left, farmhouse on the right, mud all over the place. A man in a boiler suit – the farmer, presumably – walking between the two sides.

I park, and head through the gateway, onto the moor, along a drystone wall that is covered in blotches of flat lichen in an endless array of greys, like a map etched onto the granite. The hawthorn trees still have berries on, and each branch is edged with raindrops like little diamonds.

Tarka and I walk along and down into the Scad Brook valley. It is dotted with small hawthorns and birch trees, with the odd holly as well. Normally I would walk along the Glaze Brook but it is too wet. The ground is completely saturated. So, we head uphill and along an old track before descending again to join the Glaze Brook further upstream to find the waterfall.

As we go downhill, I see a striking, vivid-green patch of vegetation. It is juniper haircap, a type of evergreen moss, masses of little green multi-armed stars clustering over the ground – an unusual sign of life in the midst of winter.

Tarka and I carry on down to the Glaze Brook, where there is a herd of miserable-looking but very handsome black and brown cattle on the other side. They are drenched. We are now in a little wood of oak and beech that surrounds the river, and the ground is covered with leaf litter. The cattle look out of place. Perhaps they feel sheltering under the trees is more important than having grass to eat.

We head upstream and – suddenly – here is the waterfall. Below it is the oval pool. The rope is still here. The waterfall crashes in one long swoop down into the water below. I climb up the side of it, looking down on the water thundering into the pool, feeling its energy, the thousands of tiny bubbles, coming off it.

There is a clearing by the waterfall, with the remains of an old blowing house, where they once smelted tin. Big blocks of granite are all covered in bright-green moss. I now realise the track I came up on probably led here in the old days; people walked along it to work. I can imagine what it must have been like then. A hive of activity, and at the centre of it a furious fire; people working away in this remote spot.

And now it is so quiet. There is no one here but me and my dog and a few cattle. I look over at the spot where Felix sat, ten years ago, watching his mother and other middle-aged women frolicking around in the waterfall. I can recall him sitting there, I can almost see him there. It is a kind of comfort, and yet . . . here I am alone, on this dreary January Saturday morning and nothing is going to bring him back.

But I'm glad I've made this small pilgrimage.

17 June

Dearest darling Felix, I feel so low. So heavily burdened, so sad. Everything feels like a massive effort. I don't want to talk to anyone or have to do anything.

I went up to the Green Hill to be with you. The willow at the entrance was bursting forth in a spurt of growth, fountains of greenery exploding upwards. Your grave was a great stand of grasses blowing in the wind, with buttercups, herb Robert, plantain, cutleaf geranium and chickweed all growing.

I brought you my first posy of sweet peas from the garden – the first ones I have ever grown. I sowed them as seeds back in January and have nurtured them all this time. Their sweet scent filled the car as I drove to see you. I placed them on your headstone, their soft, salmon-pink petals a gentle contrast to the dark slate. Flowers for my beautiful boy.

As I wake up, I am aware of a storm, a summer storm. It is lashing the house, coming and going, sometimes in sideways drifts moving fast, horizontally, past the windows, sometimes in vertical daggers crashing down on the earth. I wonder, where is Felix? I feel desperate: I have lost him again, I cannot find him. The only thing I feel I can do is go out and look, go to places where there might be a connection. Those places are around the River Dart near where he now rests.

I head out into the storm. I want to be out in the elements, raging, Lear-like, wailing and howling among the forces of nature. I park at a layby on a road that leads down to Dartmeet, and set off along a narrow, winding, grassy path through the bracken, which is high and green, covering this hillside above the river. Soon the path peters out, and I have to bushwhack my way through the bracken, much of it new, acid-green growth. Tarka, at my heels, struggles to get through it. The rain is falling constantly and soon my legs are completely sodden. Tarka sticks to me like a limpet, not knowing the terrain and also not able to see ahead, being completely dwarfed by the vegetation.

I can scream as much as I want to, out here in the rain and the wind and this sea of bracken running riot all over the hillside.

At one point it gets quite ridiculous. We are stumbling around in waist-high bracken, like a green ocean of waves as far as the eye can see, with no sign of a path at all. I wonder what on earth I'm doing here.

Then I think, *This is what my life is like: struggling to find a way through impregnable surroundings with no path to follow, not knowing when or if I will get there, what I will find at the end, if I will fall down on the way.*

But we persist. I want to find a 'settlement' that's marked on the map. I weave around, constantly checking the OS app to see where we are, until I guess we're in the right place. Suddenly, a path appears and the bracken thins out. Then I see what looks like a wall. It is very distinct: a man-made construct in the middle of nowhere. Then, more walls, with small hawthorn and rowan trees growing out of them at crazy angles. I wander around, finding five enclosures. One wall seems to incorporate two hut circles: medieval people perhaps using the buildings of their distant ancestors? There are also two very prominent large stones which look as though they may have been plundered from a stone circle – they, too, now reside in one of the walls. Was this a medieval village like the famous one at Hound Tor, nearby? I'm not sure. With that one, you can really imagine the little dwellings – you can see fireplaces for example. That's not the case here.

Here, I am not 'finding' Felix. But I sense a connection to the past, to *my* past, to these people; I feel something here. How did they manage to live, here, on this exposed hillside? I wander around, not really noticing the rain and wind any more.

Next, I want to get down to the river. There's a path that looks promising: it's good and wide, and heading in the right direction. But it ends at a drystone wall beyond which is private land enclosing Rowbrook Farm. This is the location for one of Dartmoor's best-known legends, that of Jan Coo, another young man who was taken too soon.

The story goes that Jan was a farmhand at Rowbrook Farm, and kept hearing someone calling him from the direction of the river down below. Twice he went off to the river in the dead of night to investigate, convinced someone was in distress. But he found no one. The third time, he never returned, taken, so they say, by the pixies.

As Tarka and I start to descend towards the river, bushwhacking again as there is no path, I think about Jan Coo as I hear the sounds of the river below me. It's like a sighing, a voice, a soul down there. I remember one time, walking with Felix along another part of the same river, when we became convinced there was someone sitting by the river with a radio playing. It sounded like chattering conversation up ahead of us. But there was no one there. It was just the sound of the river.

It is hard going and I start to sweat, despite the rain and wind. Ahead I see the edge of the ancient wood, which surrounds the Dart like the thicket of thorns surrounding Sleeping Beauty. Dark-green, smooth oak leaves greet us at eye height as we approach the wood, drawing us in and then over moss-covered granite boulders that litter the entire hillside. It is wet and slippery and I am now very hot as I slither, hop and jump my way down to the river, finally seeing the Dart foaming and churning below, a wall of sound as well as a wall of water. It is imposing: rushing, swelled with rain. It's a relief to be on a path again, even though it's still hard work. There are boulders to climb over, lots of slippery surfaces, but it is still a path, and I know where it is going and where I will end up.

Familiar great blocks of granite appear along the river bank, bordering rolling waterfalls with slower areas of water at the edge – areas the Dart doesn't normally reach. The river is boiling over, in spate. I find a monumental block to sit on, overlooking the torrent below. Honour dictates I should swim, though I am not that keen – the water is brown and slightly opaque. But I feel I should immerse, and so I do. I'm already wet, anyway. I take off my clothes and gingerly lower myself into a little pool to the side of the torrent, where I float about under a tree.

Afterwards, I sit for a while by the river, but start to get cold. I am also very tired. Tarka and I carry on upstream, and then, what joy – bright-orange joy! We find a little clump of chanterelles, a small satisfaction and reward for all our tramping about.

By the sea again

5 September

I'm back in Cornwall, darling, where we had so many happy holidays. Again, of course, you are missing. This year, we're in a different house. Much humbler than the one we used to go to, but still in an ideal position right by the beach.

If you were still alive, you would be a couple of years out of university. I wonder what you would be doing? And how would the pandemic have affected you? You might well have been living at home, I suspect.

Once again, I have brought your picture with us in a frame, and put it in a prominent place in the sitting room. We will bring you offerings all week. I've already found a couple of cowrie shells, which are there in pride of place.

I remember a sunny afternoon here, a few years before you died, spent looking for cowries on the beach below Nare Point. We walked out from the cottage – you, me, Dad, Lucian, Ned, Kate, Tess, Ruby and Cosy. Past the houses, with their familiar names – Salve, The Rose on the Cliff, Gillan Cove House – to the coast path, and followed it along the top of the cliffs, occasionally stopping to pick blackberries. We arrived at Nare Point, passing the Coastwatch station, and scrambled down the rocks to the cove.

There, we silently crawled around on the rocky shore, looking for the elusive shells. The sun was warm on our backs, and the sea lapped in the background, slowly but surely creeping up the beach. We were soon keeping competitive tallies of the numbers found. As the tide gradually covered the rocks, we were squashed into a smaller and smaller area of the beach.

That absorbing activity, going back to my childhood, and in turn to my mother's, in a different part of Cornwall, is a family tradition handed down. And now, when I find a cowrie, I feel a little stab of hope, a small ray of sunshine entering my heart. Maybe heaven is a place full of cowrie shells.

It is lovely to be back on the creek. I leave the house for a swim at about 8 a.m. It is cold and cloudy. Everything is shades of grey, brown, lilac and mauve – the mauve is the hydrangeas, garden escapees, that grow on the cliff above the water. It is overcast, and the sea is sludge-coloured. There are pigeons and crows on the beach, and a feeling of unremitting subduedness. The rocks are hard and slippery underfoot, and the water is daunting; its colour is unattractive and opaque. I wade in, and then take the plunge. Actually, the water is surprisingly warm and

I swim along in the gloom, just enjoying the wash of the sea on my skin and being weightless. I am enjoying it here, alone in the water, surrounded only by boats. I spot a small vessel, *Tarka of Gillan*, and swim over to her, giving her a pat, before heading across the bay and back to the beach.

Lucian tells me he and the girls swam in the dark last night and there was bioluminescence. This goes against everything I thought I knew about the required conditions. The sea is murky and choppy at the moment, and it's been cold and windy. I thought you needed a period of warm weather, stillness and clear water.

So that night, after dinner, a little drunk, I venture out alone into the darkness; no one wants to come with me. I fumble for the gate latch in the dark, and hear the sea nearby, moaning and sighing.

I walk out to the beach and cannot believe my eyes. The waves are breaking in peals of light. I've read about this, but never seen it. On and on they unfurl in dazzling arcs on the beach, glittering like diamonds.

I dip a foot in and there's an explosion of light as I do so — a great cloud of silvery brightness from which individual silver sparks fly out in the water like tiny diamonds. I swim out, overwhelmed by the animation of microscopic beings all around me. I think back to previous years at this beach, night swimming, but the display has never been as dramatic as this. The water must be bristling with tiny creatures. I feel as though I'm with Felix, that he is present in these diamond lights. It feels like swimming in outer space, here in this endless darkness, endless water, and endless, streaming lights.

The next day it is very foggy but the wind has dropped. Everything is murky again. I have an early swim in the silent grey of the creek, the only sound the gentle ploshing of small waves on the shore, and the occasional chug of a dinghy, heard not seen.

But an hour later the scene is totally different. The sun has come out, all the fog has burned off, and the sea is suddenly blue and clear. Alex and I walk to the cove at Nare Point. The tide is nearly low and we pass vast expanses of reef, colonised by herons, egrets and oyster-catchers. We are hot by the time we get to the cove and I get in the water. I can't believe how clear it is, considering the weather of the last few days.

I swim over and through a seaweed forest – vast ribbons of shiny kelp swaying in the swell, with what seem to be great flowers floating at the surface on tall, thick stems. There are other, more delicate seaweeds with silver-grey fronds, and purple algae that clusters over rocks. Thong weed, like mermaid's tresses, floats horizontally on the surface in great swathes. Every so often there is a clearing in the forest below me – a white, sandy space with curved ridges, dotted with white clam shells and the occasional swift, brown silhouette of a small wrasse swimming by. How magical is this liminal world between the deep sea and the shore?

Two oystercatchers fly by just over the surface, at my eye level, looking like children's toys with their precise, almost machine-marked black-and-white plumage, and their bright-orange beaks and legs.

A shout wakes me from my reverie. It is Lucian, arriving at the cove on a kayak. He gets out and I help him drag the boat ashore. We spend some time sitting around and then looking for cowries. He leaves in the boat, Alex leaves on foot, and I stay on.

I lie down on the warm rocks and think of all the happy times on this beach. I remember the boys lying on their tummies on the flat grey pebbles, and them jumping off the rocks at high tide. I remember finding a crystal jellyfish here with Tess. I remember Ned's dogs getting overexcited on the shore while he swam. I remember my darling Felix being here. Yes, he was here several times on this beach, on these rocks, searching for cowries as I'm doing today. I sense his spirit here, and feel I am spending time with him in this tiny cove hidden away on the South Cornwall coast.

8 September

I am in bed, thinking about the day. Alex, Lucian and I were on the beach together. I really felt your absence. You were missing. I felt sad, but I now accept that you have gone. It hurts me to say this because it seems wrong or disloyal, but there is only so long that you can rail against reality. You are gone from this earthly world at least, though who knows about the rest. Except, in a way, you are not gone. You are here in the grey stones on that beach, in the oystercatchers that flew past me — their piping call echoing across the water — in the seal that popped up earlier off the shore, its smooth head shining in the sun.

It's mizzling as I drag the kayak down the beach. It's about 8 a.m. High water is at 8:20, and I'm going to paddle up to the head of Gillan Creek.

By the sea again

For the first time in a few days, the water is pale-green and clear. I bear left around a small, rocky headland, heading upriver. As I round the corner, I see a group of egrets perched on trees overhanging the water. They stand there, hunched, like members of a choir in white cassocks. They sense my presence, and start to get the jitters. One flies off, its feet dangling like yellow boots, swiftly followed by the rest. A white feather falls from one of the birds as it takes off and lands on the surface of the water in front of me. It is pristine-white. I paddle over and pick it up. I feel it is a sign. I stow the feather safely in the kayak, to present to Felix's picture on my return.

I turn up the creek, which is like a tunnel of green. Oaks crowd the banks, and the water is the colour of pine. I pass a large fallen tree with a pair of sandpipers on it. Their call is a sort of musical gunfire: a rapid *peep-peep-peep!*

I love this quiet: the only sounds the birds and the gentle plosh of my paddle. I love the isolation, too. It's just me here in this place, which has probably looked like this for thousands of years.

At the top of the creek, the water opens out into a round shape like a lake. On one side, two rather elegant old boats are rotting. A large oak tree spreads out over the water like a tent and I paddle in through a gap in its boughs, entering a secret green space, looking out from behind its frilly leaves.

After a few quiet moments in my green tent, I turn and let the tide carry me back down. I hear the croak of a crow and look up to see it mobbing a kestrel. This goes on for a while until the kestrel gets fed up and, with a couple of aggressive dives at the crow, sends it on its way.

★

I've never been a fan of Praa Sands with its ugly housing, tatty shops and great man-made boulders lining the top of the beach. But here I am, as the majority want to go bodyboarding.

Bodyboarding has been such a feature of family holidays – since my own childhood, with my mum and my three brothers, Matthew, James and Ned, on the North Cornwall coast, starting out when we were little, in the 1970s, on wooden boards, progressing to poly-styrene and plastic ones as technology changed; as a parent myself, riding the waves with Alex, Felix and Lucian; and with my adult brothers and my nieces Tess, Ruby and Cosy. The joy and exhilaration of it have always united us.

I let the waves crash over me as I walk through them with my board to get to the spot where I want to be. I stand there waiting for the perfect one. It approaches, light refracting through the barrel, and I push off and am pro-pelled forward, shooting up the beach on a tiny amount of water. In that short moment on my board, I'm poised in a time between childhood and adulthood, between being a child and being a parent, between being alive and being dead.

After a while, I have had enough, and I set off towards the western end of the beach, where I can see an interesting-looking reef. There is still an hour before low tide, so time to explore. I pick my way across the boulders, stepping through rock pools, where the odd blenny darts aside at my approach. I can see a large, dark stone stack, very rectangular, close to the cliff. I want to get to it but can't see how. Then I see an area of smooth grey rock, which I climb over to get nearer.

Every so often I see plump anemones lodged in crevices. They look like exposed bodily orifices: red and shiny and raw. Suddenly, there is a hollow with a clear pool full of pebbles, and then, right above me, looms the stack. The rocks glisten in a muscular fashion, and then I see a very large snakelocks anemone, green and purple, open underwater like a flower, flowing and soft. Suddenly I feel as though I am inside a body, inside a great gullet or oesophagus or stomach, inside life and mortality itself. It's a sort of intense feeling of being alone – part of life, part of death, part of the mystery of the physicality of our existence. Is Felix part of that mystery of physicality? I think so. He is as real and mysterious as that craggy rock face covered with limpets and barnacles, which is crazily, physically there, and yet what does it mean to exist, to be present in the world, like that rock stack?

15 October

Oh sweetie, I've been feeling stuck and . . . Meh. Another winter is approaching without you. I miss you so much, I will never stop missing you; when I'm doing the washing-up, when I'm in the supermarket, when I'm in the bath, when I'm falling asleep, when I'm waking up, you are a part of me, a part I've lost. And yet I do carry you with me – you are present to me in all I do, in the places I go, when I'm dead-heading, when I'm looking for my keys, when I'm grating Cheddar, when I'm sitting on the sofa watching TV and knitting. I hold you, strong in me, although your loss is like a terrible gash through my soul, a slice taken out of my heart.

I decide to head over to St Mary's Bay in Brixham, which I haven't visited in years. Getting there is always a bit of a pain. You have to drive through a seemingly endless suburb with lots of twiddly bits of road until eventually you end up on a narrow, potholed lane edged with red mud from the local soil.

St Mary's Bay is looking beautiful; the sea is like a mirror and the cave-filled, red-and-grey cliffs spread as far as the eye can see. The headland just south of the bay is called Sharkham Point, and I realise I've never walked around it before. I start to follow the path, which is very close to the sea. I keep getting tantalising glimpses of the water, which is a deep jade colour. I emerge onto a grassy area above the cliff and see a little path heading down to the left. Then I see a small gate in the fence. I go through it and follow another path, down to a large group of rocks like a multi-levelled platform right on the water. I stand looking down on a labyrinth of gullies, channels and little islets offshore, clustered around an emerald-green lagoon. It has a similar feeling to the lagoon I found just a few weeks after Felix died.

I climb down and find an enormous slab of rock sloping down to the water like a ready-made ramp. To one side is a huge, flat wall of rock, perpendicular to the water, with a little hole at the bottom. Every few minutes the hole belches out large, noisy sprays of water, as though an indignant sea monster is trapped behind the rock. The water is calm, and I get in and swim, and it is so beautiful – so warm and clear and green – and I can see rocks and barnacles and red seaweed beneath me without the need for goggles. I swim out of the lagoon into the open sea through a gap in the rocks. It feels like going through some celestial portal into the next world. The water stretches out before me, limitless.

After, I walk a little further along the coast and stop and sit in a grassy nook tucked into a steep-sided cliff looking over to the next beach, Mansands, which has the sun on it. Below me is the sea, still flat and jade, and there are more small rock islands just off the shore – red sandstone covered with splashes of white guano. Gulls are clustered all over the islands.

The guano reminds me of a time my friend Matt and I did a rather epic swim from very near here. We swam from St Mary's Bay along the coast to Durl Rock, which is a long finger of stone that sticks out into the sea and looks like a person lying on their back having a sleep. It was a day similar to this, with lovely flat sea. We felt a sense of excitement as we moved away from the bay and swam alongside the red-layered cliffs, and past caves and inlets. It wasn't arduous, but it was long. It took us about forty-five minutes to get to Durl Rock, and we passed many islets covered in guano along the way. Oh, the stink! I'll never forget it – it was an animal, fishy, fleshy smell.

That was about a decade ago. Felix was about fifteen at the time, I guess. God, how little we knew then. Life was normal, with the usual family tensions, happy times, bad times, scrapping along. We were oblivious to the bombshell that was going to drop just a few years later.

What do I think about it all now? I accept it. It is real; I am in no doubt about that. It's a hard fact, just as hard as the rock I've just been scrambling about on, as true as the sea spreading out before me, as existent as the reflection of the evening sunlight dappling the water, as the fly that has just buzzed past my nose.

The question is always, *What do I do with that reality?* It can't be dealt with, sorted. It just has to be lived with. I still find it very hard to accept, but I have. I know he is dead. And yet the horror of that is still so real, so cruel, like the dark night of a relentless storm.

Sitting here on the rock, I watch a trawler steaming out to sea. Gradually it moves into the distance, heading for the horizon, disappearing from view.

Epilogue

I am back at the green hill, far away.

A warm wind touches me as I stand by Felix's grave, looking at the River Dart winding along below. The tide is high and the river is full. In a few hours, it will be reduced to mud. And then, after another few hours of creeping water, it will be full again.

It is just before dusk. The last of the pink light is fading and a smoky, misty greyness is descending. The sea is the faintest blue smudge. This is the end and also the beginning. I shiver slightly.

I remember my first, agonised visits here. Standing in a catatonic state, felled by the enormity of what had happened. Feeling out of my body, out of time, floating in a whirl of senseless thought and feeling – the pain was so

great that I almost couldn't feel it. It was like being anaes-
thetised, knocked out by an event that was both
incomprehensible and incredible; a loss of sensation, and, at
the same time, an excess of sensation, so much so that it felt
like something else, something never before experienced.

Gradually the anaesthetic has worn off. I feel everything now. Some days I feel it very intensely. Other days it
is in the background. But it is always there.

I leave the burial ground and head for the river. I push
open the gate and walk down the decaying wooden walk-
way until I'm at the water's edge. The leaves around me
are on the turn, shades of brown and grey, and the occasional flash of orange. I walk along beside the wizened
oaks that guard the water, until I reach North Quay.

The light continues to recede, and I hear an owl hoot
from the other side of the river. The sound drifts and
fades. Another owl calls in response.

A few minutes later, and it is dark. It is just me and the
owls and the Dart, and Felix, up in his grave on the Green
Hill. I lie down on the flat, grassy top of the quay and look
at the sky. The grass feels cold and damp beneath my back.
My breathing slows.

I think about the river, emptying out into the sea, into
a kind of eternity. And I think about Ariel's song in *The
Tempest*:

> Full fathom five thy father lies.
> Of his bones are coral made;
> Those are pearls that were his eyes;
> Nothing of him that doth fade
> But doth suffer a sea-change
> Into something rich and strange.

Epilogue

And then I'm back in the school hall in Torquay, watching Felix in a performance of *A Midsummer Night's Dream*. He's about fifteen, I think, wearing an old smock of mine that I potato-printed at school in the 1970s, and long wooden beads, because they've set the play in the days of Flower Power. Playing Demetrius, he runs onto the stage, pursued by Hermia. He declaims passionately: 'Do I entice you? Do I speak you fair? Or, rather, do I not in plainest truth tell you, I do not, nor I cannot love you?' The emotion is youthfully intense, and he is very convincing. I can see him so vividly on that stage, running back and forth, with Helena in hot pursuit. My young, beautiful, earnest son, imagining that adult, romantic love that he would never get to experience.

The cold and damp are penetrating my back now. I get up and undress. I climb down the hard, steel rungs of the ladder at the end of the quay, and sink backwards into the water with a gentle splash that echoes across the surface. I start to move, feeling warm trickles over my skin, my body wet, and my mind dissolving.

The trickles of water run across me and down, down, away, down the river and away to the sea.

As I move, tiny white diamonds stream from my hands, arms and legs. They dance, lighting up the blackness of the river. Millions of microscopic creatures are in the water, glowing with life and light. It's like swimming in space, swimming through the stars, into the dark night above.

The moon appears, huge and white and heavy in the sky.

I feel a sense of rightness. I am winding back to something private, fundamental, and at the same time universal. I am losing myself, falling back into my genes, into atoms, into matter, fading into dust. I am entering somewhere else – somewhere, perhaps, where Felix is.

Acknowledgements

This book is, of course, dedicated to our beloved son and brother Felix, and I want to thank everyone who knew and loved him in his short life. I could not have written it without the love and backing of my husband Alex and son Lucian. They have had to deal with their own pain as well as coping with the idea of me writing about it. Thank you.

Special mention must go to my darling friend Giovanna Mallucci, who came to my rescue, late at night, on that hideous day in Leicester when, hundreds of miles from home, I discovered that Felix had died. Thank you also to Vanessa Cluett who dropped everything and drove her up from London that night. Giovanna, we've been friends for the last forty years, and have been there for each other on our darkest days, as well as our happiest. Your friendship means everything.

My parents-in-law, Paul and Lesley Murdin, have been an enormous support as well as being incredibly generous in becoming patrons of the book. My thanks also to my old friend from my dim and distant schooldays, Euan Craik, who is also a patron; what a wonderful, kind gesture for which I am so grateful, as indeed I am to all the lovely people who pledged for the book.

Judy Gordon-Jones, Yaara Lahav Gregory and Anna Lunk from my writers' group in Ashburton were so helpful during the writing process, as well as supplying what must amount to gallons of tea over the years. I am also indebted to Tanya Shadrick – who has been a tower of support, and who helped me improve the opening pages – and to Sarah Perry for her kindness and encouragement. My nieces Tess Tallulah, Ruby Rainbow and Cosy Blossom created a stunning initial cover for the book at the crowdfunding stage, and I've been honoured to include Ruby's prizewinning poem in it. My dear friends Matt Newbury and Aaron Kitts warmly offered me a room in their home on the sunny English Riviera whenever I needed to get away and concentrate (fuelled by the finest white wine, of course). Mathew Clayton and Alex Eccles at Unbound brought the book into the world with skill and sensitivity.

I would also like to thank all the wonderful people at the small charity SUDEP Action for the love and support they give to those bereaved by epilepsy, and for their tireless work towards understanding what causes SUDEP, and making life safer for those with epilepsy.

To my friends both near and far: what would I do without you? Huge gratitude to you all, in no particular order: Felix's godparents Sean Klein and Sandra Symons. Camilla Forbes, Anna Dunscombe, Ellie Ricketts, Judy Marshall, Rachel Dawson, Catherine and Alex Rees-Stephan, Ben Bradshaw and Neal Dalgleish, Clare Hetherington, Stephanie Horton, Trixie Rawlinson, Esther White and Clare Pettinger. Love and thanks also to the Sunday morning swim gang: Sally Sutton, Angie Watson, Jo and Rob Feloy, Kathrin Deutsch, Karen Pearson, Rebecca Beattie and Jude Cranmer.

My darling sisters-in-law Kate and Louisa have been absolutely solid in the years since Felix's death, talking about

Acknowledgements

him regularly and remembering his birthday and anniversaries. You two are true sisters. My brothers Matthew, James and Ned have always been there for me. Finally, although my parents are both dead, I want to mention them. If Felix's death has taught me anything, it is that we carry our special people with us always. Roger and Bennie, I wish you were still here and miss you every day.

Illustrations

Illustrations

The old stones: Langstone Moor stone circle, Dartmoor
The suitcase: Tristis Rock, Dartmoor
The virus: Thurlestone Rock, Devon
Hoar frost: Giant's Marble, Dartmoor
A storm: Glaze Brook waterfall, Dartmoor
By the sea again: cowrie shells
Epilogue: River Dart viewed from the Green Hill
Acknowledgements: a portrait of Felix

A note on the author

Sophie Pierce is a writer and broadcaster who lives on the edge of Dartmoor in Devon, where she loves to swim in rivers, lakes and the sea. For many years she worked for the BBC as a radio and TV reporter. She is the co-author, with Matt Newbury, of *Wild Swimming Torbay*, *Wild Swimming Walks Dartmoor and South Devon*, *Wild Swimming Walks Cornwall* and *Wild Swimming Walks Dorset and East Devon*.

Unbound is the world's first crowdfunding publisher, established in 2011.

We believe that wonderful things can happen when you clear a path for people who share a passion. That's why we've built a platform that brings together readers and authors to crowdfund books they believe in — and give fresh ideas that don't fit the traditional mould the chance they deserve.

This book is in your hands because readers made it possible. Everyone who pledged their support is listed below. Join them by visiting unbound.com and supporting a book today.

With special thanks to Euan Craik and Paul and Lesley Murdin, patrons of this book

Adrian Abbotts
Jane Acton
Marissa Acton
Caroline Adams
Aine Allen
Lisa Allen
Justin Althaus
Rachel Anderson
Carl Ape
Laura Arcand

Alicia Arce
Ruth Arnold
Eileen Ashcroft
Jonathan
   Aspinwall
Sian Niamh
   Astley
Paul Baggaley
Louise Banks
Louise Barber

Max Barker
Pauline Barker
Jo Barley
Rosie Barnfield
Iona Barr
Kate Barton
Alice Baxter
Cat Beech
Mark Beeson
Sanchia Berg

Supporters

Hannah Best
Fiona Bettles
Stephen Biggs
Alice Bird
Lucy Bird
Sarah Bird
Hannah
  Blanchford
Amanda Blande
Amanda Bluglass
Robert Bluglass
Jo Booth
Casey Bottono
Julia Bovee
Ben Bradshaw
Benjamin
  Bradshaw
Una Brandreth
Andy Brereton
Anne Brichto
Jane Brown
Gilly Butterworth
Claire Callender
Rupert Callender
Joanna Carr
Holly Cartlidge
Barbara
  Challender
Lesley Chapman
Anne Charles
Emma Chetwynd
  Stapylton

Jan Chetwynd
  Stapylton
Polly Chetwynd
  Stapylton
Lucy Clare
Vanessa Cluett
Philippa Coates
Deborah
  Cochrane
Tonia Collett
Denise Collins
Alan Connett
Emily Cooke
Harry Cooke
Andy Corsham
Dino Costa
Louise Crathorne
Cressida Craufurd
Helen Currell
Deborah Curtis
Stéphanie
  d'Haussy
Neal Dalgleish
Annette Daly
Dana and Ron
Juliana Dart
James Davenport
Nigel Davies
Rachel Dawson
Leo Devine
Simon Lee Dicker
Judith Dimant

Belinda Dixon
Josie Dixon
Cathy Dobson
Lou Doret
Karen Dossett
Stuart Driver
Lesley Duncan
Hilary Dunlop
Rosalyn Dunn
Anna Dunscombe
Bea Dunscombe
Vincent Eames
jimmy@
  beyondgoodbye.
  co.uk Edmonds
Charlotte Ellis
Kirk England
Amanda Evans
Cawston Family
Jo Feloy
Stacey Fennell
Niki Fforde
Mark Findlater
Jenny Findlay
Gail Fogarty
Ella Foote
Camilla Forbes
Jeremy Fowler
Robin Franklin
Martha Frase
Lynne French
Sally Friedman

Supporters

George Furnival
Kari Furre
Mrs Joanna
  Garner
Norman Gold
Jo-Ann Gonsalves
Charlotte Goodlet
Judy Gordon Jones
Catherine Gough
Rebecca Green
Gerard Greenway
Daniella Gregory
Timothy Gregory
Rachael Haggan
Kirsty Hale
Kathrin Hall
Jeff Hamaoui
Sara Hamilton
Emma
  Handscombe
James
  Handscombe
Louisa
  Handscombe
Issy Hardman
Robyn Hardyman
Matt Harvey
Tarra Hassin
Lisa Hay
Sharon Heather
Liz Hedge
James Hedger

Alison Heimann
Amanda
  Hembrough
Patrick Hennessy
Heather Henry
Emunah Herzog
Clare
  Hetherington
Philip Hewitt
Beverley High
James
  Hodge-Brooks
Ann Hogan
Tess Holmes
Stephanie Horton
Cressida Hudson
Sara Hurley
Jo Irving
Cathryn Ives
Pippa Jackson
Jane James
Sarah James
Edwin Janes
Rowland Janes
Lisa Jeffery
Nina Jeffries
Sally Jenkins
Mark Jessett
Alison Johns
Karin Jordan
Rachael Jowitt
Caroline Joyce

Sarah Kafala
Christina Kennedy
Helen Kennedy
Debs Kerr
Dan Kieran
Sean Klein
Diana Knight
Nichola Knight
Andrzej
  Kosmaczewski
Edith La Mache
Robin Lacey
Hadas Lahav
Yaara Lahav
  Gregory
Jemima Laing
Ruth Lamont
Jenny Landreth
Julie Lang
Debbie Lannon
Cordelia Law
Sofie Layton
Nicki Ledgard
Michele Legg
Nora Levine
Helen Lewis
Jill Lewis
Ju Lewis
Tracey Lewis
Emily Lezzeri
Judith Liddell-
  King

Supporters

Patrick Limb
Louise Lindsay
Helen Locke
Ruth Longfellow
Sophie Lovett
Virginia Low
Ben Lowings
Karen Lubbe
David Lubin
Anna Lunk
Katie Lusty
Louise MacAllister
Allan Macfadyen
Serena Mallinson
Giovanna Mallucci
Patrick Mallucci
Candida March
Ben March and
    Bryonie Hopper
Laura Marchant-
    Short
Judy Marshall
Ariadna Martin
Queenie Martin
Rebecca Mason
Amanda
    Masterson
Stephen Matthews
Chris Mattison
Zoe May
Lawrence
    McCrossan

Elma Andrew
    McGoldrick
Tamsin Melville
Jody Merelle
Lucinda
    Middleton
Vanessa Miles
Roberta Mitchell
John Mitchinson
Linda Monckton
Stella Moore
Sally Morgan
Georgina Morley
Matt Mulcrone
Alex Murdin
Benedict Murdin
Lucian Murdin
Peta Myers
Hugh Nankivell
Carlo Navato
Judith Naylor
Patrick Naylor
Aidan Neligan
Rebecca Nelsey
Matt Newbury
Verity Nicholls
Sue Nightingale
Deb Norman
Pamela O'Connor
Morag Orr
Inga Page
Olivia Palmer

Alberthe Papma
Jan Parnell
Hannah Pearce
Jeremy Pearce
Angela Peard
Karen Pearson
Nicola Peck
David Pendleton
David Perry
Sarah Perry
Clare Pettinger
Christine Pfaff
Liz Phillips
Sam Pickett
Matthew Pierce
Amy Plowman
Esme Podmore
Justin Pollard
Mike Porteous
Lucie Potter
Richard Povall
Rosie Powell
Suzy Price
Sarah Prince
Emma Pugh
Emma Pusill
    (Plum Duff)
Steve Race
Sarah Ransome
Trixie Rawlinson
Catherine and Alex
    Rees Stephan

Supporters

Philip Reeve
Elizabeth Richards
Emma Richards
Daniel Ricketts
Ellie Ricketts
Rachel Ritchie
Kate Robarts
Gilly Robinson
Ben Rogers
Mike Roper
Adam Royle
Gemma Ruffle
Laura K Ruiz
Kate Russell
Paul & Val Russell
Sheila Russell &
    Bill Lakin
Audrey Ryder
Caroline Sale
Ursula Salter
Claire Sampson
Christoph Sander
Michele Sandhu
Amar Sangha
Ali Sargent
Orla Savage
Natalie Savona
Guy Saward
Rud Sawers
Gillian
    Scarborough
Sarah Scott

Suzanne Scott
    Wilson
William Searle
Fiona Senior
Jane Seymour
Tanya Shadrick
Lenny Shallcross
Claire Sharp
Caroline Shea
Helen Shelley
Cliff Shephard
Pam Shepherd
Sharky Siân
Johanna Sidey
Stephanie Simon
Fiona Sinclair
Jane Slaughter
Paul Smith
Amy Snowden
Sandra Solomides
Boni Sones
Tom Speight
Tanya Spilsbury
Daniel Start
Julian Stern
Kate Stone
Kate Strasdin
Rachel Sumaria
Jack Surtees
Jenny Suttie
Rachel Sutton
Sally Sutton

Stuart Sweeney
Jaine Swift
Gillian Taylor
Neil Taylor
Christian Teasdel
Maxine Theobald
Katie Thompson
Laura Thompson
Pamela Thurgood
Harriet Todhunter
Debbie Travers
Susan Tyler
Boo Tyrrell
Susan Valentine
Jackie Vans-
    Colina
Annie Vincent
Sally Wace
Jacquie Wain
Roz Walker
Barbara Wallis
Isobel Waterhouse
Ms Catherine
    Waters
Sally Watkins
Angie Watson
David Watson
James Watts
Alison Waylen
Lynne Welsh
Carole Whelan
Esther H White

Supporters

Sarah White
Miranda Whiting
Emma Widdis
Alison Williams
Heather Williams
Suzy Williamson

Chris Willis
Martin Willitts
Christopher
  Wilson
Sara Wilson
Izzy Woolrych

Claudia
  Wordsworth
Rhiannon
  Yarranton
Oliver Yates
Caroline Yorston